Caught in the Middle

A collection of short stories from a sixth grade teacher and her own experiences that enhance the classroom.

Deborah Burggraaf

Communications

©2008 Deborah Burggraaf
All rights reserved

ISBN 978-0-9818990-3-9
Library of Congress Control Number 2008938634

No part of this book may be reproduced, stored in a retrieval system, or transmitted in any form or by any means, electronic, mechanical, photocopying, recording, or otherwise without the written permission of the author.

Published
By
Protective Hands Communications
Riviera Beach, FL 33404
Phone: 561-841-4990
Toll free: 866-540-9959
www.protectivehands.com
info@protectivehands.com

Printed in the United States

TABLE OF CONTENTS

TABLE OF CONTENTS

FOREWORD

I have been teaching grade six for over a decade. But one morning in January of 2008, I had become one of my students for the very first time.

I woke up and couldn't get myself out of bed. In the bathroom, I needed assistance getting up from the toilet. I couldn't even get dressed by myself. I was now suffering from a disability just like the many students I have taught over the years. For the first time in my life, I knew what it was like to be physically challenged at many tasks that I had previously taken for granted.

I was under attack with a case of fibromyalgia coupled with two viruses that followed: Parvo B-19 and Reynaud's Syndrome. Never have I had any medical concerns, barring my tonsils being removed when I was six years old.

For the first time in my life, I knew what it was like to awake each day with a disability. True, often students are unaware of their disabilities; however, in the classroom today and at grade six level, many students know what their areas of concern are and try to make accommodations for those disabilities. Furthermore, students at the middle school level work closely with their case load manager, a teacher with Special Needs certification. These students are instructed to ask for additional time when taking tests or to ask for an additional day to complete a homework assignment. These accommodations are listed in the Individual Education Plans for the students with special needs.

Now I had special needs and needed my own set of accommodations. The administrative staff at Limestone Middle was stellar when addressing my limitations. I was issued a special parking spot adjacent to my portable. Bus Duty was cancelled and I no longer had to walk to the front office each morning; I simply emailed the principal's secretary that I was in my classroom. If I needed additional time off, even though I was out of sick days as the end of the school year approached, I was told not to worry. I had support from my principal with my special needs and I was able to complete the entire school year.

Whenever I give my students an assignment or project, I have always asked them a question, "Is this your best effort?" This question has new meaning for me. Their *best* may not in fact be the work I had expected; however, it truly may be the student's best effort for a specific task.

I now have the ability to accept and honor the work of the individual learner, though it may not be the outcomes I had anticipated, but indeed, it *is* the student's very best.

As for me, the sheets on my bed are no longer smooth and taunt. I still need scissors to open lunch meat packages and boxes of cereal bars. I still hobble side to side when I walk, and on certain days, I still need help getting dressed or lifted up from a soft chair. My life has changed with this sudden disability with which I now live.

It is perhaps the greatest lesson I have learned in life as a teacher. This book was written with one thumb from my left hand and four fingers on my right hand. The open sores on the tips of my fingers from Reynaud's are still healing. No one can tell me now that anything is impossible. Imagine, writing an entire book with limited use of hands! My students, all of my students, including the ones with disabilities, can accomplish any dream they have in life! I did it; they can do it, too!

I will open my classroom this year with one

sore remaining on the tip of my pinky finger. A setback? Yes. Will it stop me from being a good teacher? NO! I will go forward in life, as I teach my students to do. Follow your dreams in life and believe that anything you want to achieve is possible! As one former colleague from Orange Grove Middle School shares,

"There are no setbacks in life; only obstacles that challenge us."

The short stories that follow are both events from my classroom as well as people who have influenced me over the years. I chose to tell these specific stories to inspire you, to give you hope, and to share with you timeless treasures.

To each of you...the teachers of the young lives...Inspire!

Deb Burggraaf

SPECIAL ACKNOWLEDGEMENTS

I am forever thankful for the positive impact my teachers and mentors have had on me throughout my school years. Thank you Dr. Don Beard, Mr. Kim Miltzenberger, Mr. Theodore Taylor, Dr. John Kim, Dr. Pat Barnes, Ms. Faust and Ms. Zucca, Mr. Mel Schwartz, Mrs. Linda Scott, Dr. Matt Shoemaker, Dr. Elmay Hatcher, Mr. Frank Attoun and Mr. Deti, to name some of many.

A special thank you to my dear friends who have been by my side for many years and who have loved me unconditionally: Mary Rickabaugh, Sharon Bradley, Anne White, and Franny Saar. We have each shared many joys and sorrows over the years; thank you for being an important part of my life.

I would like to thank my editor and publisher, Mr. Steve White, who has made a dream of a lifetime come true for me.

It is with sincere gratitude that I extend my appreciation to Melissa Malley, for providing me with the best health care possible over the years.

With appreciation, I extend a special thank

you to Dr. Michael Sinclair and his Staff for unmatched health care and dedication to patients.

A big thank you to Mary Ann Miller Photography for the outstanding and memorable moments captured on film.

A heartfelt thank you to David Prochaska, who no longer is here on earth to celebrate this book, but would be very proud of me for finally sitting down to write it.

Warm sentiments extend to my family, my sister, Judi Ann Morley, and mother, Kathi Caram Olmstead, for always believing in me.

Finally, I would like to thank my husband, Willem, for his support and understanding while pursuing my writing dream. I thank him for his enduring love as we share our life together.

DEDICATION

This book is dedicated to David Prochaska, whose memory still lives on today.

This book is also dedicated to my students, past, present, and future. Each of you has given me more joy than you'll ever know.

Chapter 1

CHEATING

The sounds of the middle school bell ring and it's show time. Nearly thirteen hundred students navigate through the corridors and chatter is heard as they start to form lines outside of the classrooms. I greet the students and they enter the classroom and take out their agendas.

The pledge of allegiance and the announcements are broadcasted via television and some students listen, while others talk over the telecast. One student raises her hand and needs a temporary identification tag made from an index card. The classroom door opens and the Vice-Principal has requested a student be sent down to her office. Another student gets up to sharpen his pencil making moderate circular sweeps as he leans against the wall observing a girl from across the room. Suddenly, a student approaches me with a bloody nose.

"And justice for all," concludes the opening daily routine as I write the pass for Hadley, the young lady with the red-tipped nostrils clinging to tissues pressed against the tip of her nose.

"I forgot my lunch money," bursts Christian as the door closes.

"Oh, my mom wrote you a note, Mrs. Burggraaf," chimes Jodie.

I quickly write a pass for Hadley to go to the nurse's office as I collect the hand-written note from Jodie.

Being a teacher seems to be the job of a master magician. We process and deliver knowledge in subject matter and continuously juggle time. Each morning the door opens to the youthful smiling faces, with backpacks overloaded with books and binders creating fast-moving hunch-backed turtles in somewhat of a curvy line. You never know what each day will bring.

The students take out their journals and begin copying the quote for the day presented on the LCD. The room is now dark except for the bright Florida sunshine peeking through the cracks of the vertical blinds. As I walk around the classroom, I'm checking to make sure all students have their journals and pencils out. Students are seated in groups of four and there are thirty-one eager active learners writing in their journals trying to make meaning of a statement said a long time ago.

Across the room, I approach two girls looking over each other's shoulders and onto single sheets of paper. One young girl is working on a math sheet from another class and is copying the bottom half of her friend's paper onto a math worksheet with her name on it. I asked both girls what they were doing and who the work is for. They tell me the name of the math teacher and I gently state that I will make sure Mr. Stevens receives them by the end of the school day. I collect the math problems as the girls take out their journals and get on task. The Office Aide enters to collect attendance and we are now ready to share our responses to the quote.

The two girls are catching up on their writing and whispering with fretful looks on their faces. I reassure them with a tender smile and soft eyes, and they appear to be focused on the subject intended for this period. Popsicle sticks with student's names on them are pulled randomly and students share their responses to the quote. Most students are eager to share with the whole class as they anticipate going to the pink reward basket filled with stickers, erasers, and pencils.

Hadley returns from the nurse with a pass

and sits down with a zip lock bag of ice pressed against the side of her nose and asks a friend for the quote.

The vocabulary words are put on the LCD for copying and the students take out a lined, white sheet of paper and "hotdog" fold it twice creating four columns. As the students copy the ten vocabulary words into the first column, I ask Hadley how she is feeling.

"I'm okay, Mrs. Burggraaf," she says as she uses one arm to reach for a piece of paper. "Sometimes when the weather changes and it's dry out, I usually have more bloody noses," she chimes with a warm smile.

The students label their papers with name, date, period, and have their four columns identified with *Word, Picture, Definition, and Synonym*. Students work in their collaborative groups and begin to draw the meanings of each word with symbols. I look at the clock to see there is only ten minutes left to the period. We discuss the first word, and a student volunteers to share his drawing with the class. A definition is provided by a student from Team Three and everyone in class feverishly copies it down. The next five words are discussed and the clock keeps ticking. Finally, with only two minutes left in class, I instruct the students to place their vocabulary worksheets into their Language Arts folder for completion tomorrow, and ask the students to quietly wait for the dismissal bell. I also give them free "whisper talk time" the final minute before leaving.

The two girls approach me regarding their math assignments with a scornful appearance on their faces. I assured them that Mr. Stevens would receive them by the end of the day as I had planning period at two o'clock and would hand deliver them.

As usual, Mr. Stevens was greeting his students at the front door as I handed the math work to him with a pink post-it note on top.

"Brooke was writing the answers down from Melanie's paper in my class during the opening minutes," I explained. "I thought you might like to discuss this with the girls as they will want their work returned for your class today."

"Thank you, Mrs. Burggraaf." Mr. Stevens' eyebrows rose as he peered over his glasses to see me. I waved and walked off to do my copying for the following week's assignment and to check my box in the office.

The next morning, the school bell rang again

and all thirty-one students lined up outside my portable. It was on the humid side, with the Florida early morning fog burning off and bursting into a day of sunshine with clear skies. Melanie and Brooke were at the end of the long student line slowly approaching the entrance to the classroom. When they arrived, Brooke presented a gift.

"This is for you, Mrs. Burggraaf." Brooke smiled as she extended a pink rose from her youthful arm.

"And from me, too," added Melanie, with a smile behind her soft white rose.

My eyes widened with a warm smile. "Oh, what a lovely surprise! Thank you so much, girls."

Melanie said, "No, thank you, Mrs. Burggraaf, for not getting us in trouble for copying each other's homework in your class yesterday."

I asked Brooke to fill my small cup with water from the drinking fountain by the bus depot and she placed the two roses in the cup and placed them on my desk. I thought, "two roses among many..." and left it at that. I had remained calm, pointed out what was wrong in a very subtle manner, and went on with my day.

I still have those two roses pressed in wax paper in my quote book as a reminder of how to approach a problem with gentleness and compassion. The copying incident will always be a part of the learning process. The most important lesson is that students learn from a mistake, make decisions about what is right and wrong, and become better individuals from that experience.

I will continue to keep pressed flowers in my quote book.

Chapter 2

MY FIRST LOVE

I remember sitting behind Gary Tomanos in Mrs. Dagwood's sixth grade math class. Nothing else mattered in the world to me but getting off that school bus and getting to homeroom just to sit behind the most beautiful guy in the world.

I would enter the classroom filled with the hustle and bustle of the homeroom first bell and peer around students just to see if he had arrived yet. I took my seat in the back of the room, as Mrs. Dagwood had us alphabetically seated by last names. The seat in front of me was still empty.

The second bell chimed as I reached for my notebook and pencils from my green knapsack and as I placed them on top of my desk, in he walked. I lifted my desktop to hide behind it and slowly selected my favorite pink eraser as I gazed at his controlled gait as he walked down the aisle heading towards his seat.

He was perfect. He had a beautiful smile with slightly parted, sleek lips. His hair was a soft shade of brown, thin, and parted on the left side. His deep brown morsel eyes captivated anyone who caught a glance.

Gary had on his ROTC uniform today, which only made his appearance more intensified and dreamlike. It was a dark blue tightly-fitted suit with a crisp white shirt underneath. He wore a gold decorated ribbon around his left shoulder and several ornate pins adorned his left lapel above his pocket with his name. He parted his lips and said, "Good morning, Deb," as he positioned himself into his seat.

I smiled and heard nothing else. I vaguely caught Mrs. Dagwood's figure as she paced back and forth in front of the classroom in between all of the students' torsos seated in class. However, I did not hear one word.

Gary passed the math worksheet to me and I thought, "He just touched my paper..." I remember how cherished this piece of paper was to me and I'd keep it forever.

As I sat in math class, I looked at the back of his head. Nothing else mattered to me in the world. The white rim of his shirt peeked out at me bordering his Aerospace uniform and I was madly in love in sixth grade. Just to sit near Gary made the whole day worthwhile.

Suddenly, Mrs. Dagwood called on Gary to go

to the board to complete a math problem. I fidgeted with my pencil and realized that my paper was blank. The class was now on problem twelve, and all I could do was watch Gary walk to the front of the class towards the board. He had the perfect body shape, broad at the shoulders like a middle-weight fighter and tight with a firm waist to match. He was perfect and I knew in my heart that I could look at him for the rest of my life.

Gary worked his problem on the board and step-by-step I copied his white chalk answers to my paper. It was the only thing I had on my paper besides my name. As he finished the problem, he dropped the chalk on the floor and it split into two. He had to bend over to pick it up and he turned red like a tomato with embarrassment. Everyone in the class was laughing but me. Gary placed the pieces of chalk on the ledge and walked back to his seat with his eyes on me. He was beet red!

I offered a consoling smile as he took his seat. Two boys across from us started chanting, "Gary Tomato! Gary Tomato!" which only made him redder in the face.

He cocked his head slightly back towards me as if he was looking for comfort and reassur-

ance.

"Don't worry, you did a great job," I offered.

His eyes met mine with a soft "thank you" and he turned his body back into his seat.

For the rest of my days in Mrs. Dagwood's grade six math class I was lost in love. I never really liked math nor could I pay attention, so I turned out to be an "average" student. But to be in love and have the boy I was crazy about right in front of me for a whole year was worth struggling on any math problem in life.

As years have passed I've thought about him and wondered how he turned out. I phoned him once when I visited Connecticut and reintroduced myself.

"Hello, Deb...Wow, it's been years, how are you?" He remembered me! He told me that he had become a city police officer, married, with three children. He was happy and that's what mattered to me. I had my year of being captivated by him and to this day, he was my first love.

As far as math, I'll have to rely on a calculator and my financial advisor for the rest of my life. I wouldn't trade that one year in grade six behind Gary Tomanos and being in love for the success of any pre-algebra problem. Today, I can still see him in his sharp ROTC uniform striding to take his seat and smiling over me.

Chapter 3

MARIA

Maria was a quiet, thin girl, who mostly kept to herself. She had long, straggly blonde hair parted in the middle with each side swept behind her ears. She came to class with older, mismatched clothes, sometimes a yellow and blue plaid button down shirt with beige, well-worn capris. Her sneakers were old with scuff marks, perhaps reflecting the torn and tattered life only she knew.

As I got to know Maria during the school year, she opened up. With a crooked smile, she spoke softly.

"You don't want to know my life, Mrs. Burggraaf," she offered as I inquired about completing her class assignment as homework.

"My dad was crazy last night," she added, still with a smile backed with wet, glazed eyes.

"Maria, would you like to talk with someone, perhaps a guidance counselor? She's very good and can offer some strategies to help you at home," I suggested.

"It wouldn't do any good, Mrs. Burggraaf. My mom's been through this before and nothing changes...she still goes back to him." Maria was again speaking softly behind a crying voice.

Today's assignment was to write a "Dialog Poem" using one of the characters from the short story and responding with your own voice. The students made two columns on their papers and began writing direct quotes from the story as they connected with the text. In the second column, students write their responses.

As teachers, we model what we are teaching. The only concern I had is if the students were going to ask me to share my writing with the class. Today, the teacher would pass. I couldn't help myself, I needed to write about Maria. And I didn't want to reveal my poem to anyone.

Maria's Voice

"Now class, this assignment is due tomorrow."

"I didn't do the homework, Mrs. Burggraaf."

"There are no exceptions to the rule. Your only obligation is to be good students and to try your best."

"My parents had a fight last night. Dad was drinking and left."

"You've had two weeks to complete this unit."

"There are holes in the walls. He punched them and his fists were bleeding. My mom was crying."

"Don't forget a title page and table of contents."

"We can't leave though, my mom doesn't work. We have no money. My dad keeps all the money."

"Print your name, date, and period in the upper right hand corner of your papers."

"It's a nightmare Mrs. Burggraaf, living with an alcoholic. I wouldn't want you to know this."

"Pass your units to the end of your rows; they will be collected at the end of the period."

"I wouldn't wish my life on anyone."

"These will be graded and returned to you on Monday."

"I think I'm going to go live with my aunt in Virginia. She's my mom's sister."

"Remember, this unit will reflect one quarter of the semester's grade."

"I leave tomorrow, Mrs. Burggraaf. I will miss you. Can I have your number?"

"Have a nice weekend, class. Be safe."

"I will write, Mrs. Burggraaf, I will write..."

Of, course, when a student reveals concerns within the home or school, we immediately send them to talk with a counselor. By the time Maria had expressed a concern about her home, she was already planning to "get out" again and flee to her aunt's house.

After she had shared her home life with me, I continued to teach, feeling quite gloomy and lacking my normal energy level. I had felt drained and too saddened to continue my day. However, some days are like this, when we are dealt a blow and miraculously plunge forward with our lesson. After all, there are nearly thirty other students in the classroom with eager minds that deserve an effective Language Arts lesson.

To this day, I wonder how Maria is doing in this big world that we live in. Did she turn out alright? Did she follow in her mother's footsteps and end up with an abusive man? Was she strong enough to challenge herself to take a different path? Had I encouraged her enough to realize there were other routes and that she could carve her own destination?

I think of Maria now and then and pray she is successful at her chosen path in life. That was my dream for her; that she would be strong enough to pursue her own destiny.

Maria never did write to me, however, I hope she continued to write for herself. I wonder if she still wears her crooked smile.

Chapter 4

MISS ZUCCA

I was in sixth grade and my father's teachers, Ms. Faust and Ms. Zucca were now my teachers for my literature and mathematics classes. They were old teachers, but their familiarity gave me a sense of comfort.

Ms. Zucca was a tall woman with a thin frame and wide hips. Whispers of gray locks with curly bangs draped her aging forehead. She had a long nose and soft lips that matched the tone of her voice. She always wore nylons and close toed one-inch black high heel shoes.

I remember the sound of her footsteps walking through the aisles in the classroom as we worked on our assignments. I only raised my head enough to catch her glide by as she paced herself, checking our work.

Once in awhile, Ms. Zucca touched my paper to instruct me to change something or to point out a mistake. Her long fingers were wrinkled and were lined like a freeway with blue roads of veins that bubbled from her thin skin. They were caring hands with ridged, oval fingernails.

I glanced up at her tall figure once every so

often and she offered me a smile. I knew she cared. Her eyes were full of knowledge and I knew that she loved to teach us.

My favorite time in class was when she read aloud to us. She sat tall in her chair in the front of the classroom as if she were a propped puppet. She read to our class everyday, whether it was a chapter reading book, or a picture book. And Ms. Zucca loved poetry. It was only fitting that it was in her class that I developed a love for poetry.

Henry Wadsworth Longfellow, Emily Dickinson, and Edgar Allan Poe became familiar friends and profound writers in my life. She read poetry with such conviction and tone that brought each of us into the experience. We learned about human compassion, empathy, and sentiment as she read, The Family Under the Bridge, *by Natalie Savage Carlson, and* Make Way for Ducklings, *by Robert McCloskey.*

Ms. Zucca taught us metaphors and the use of symbols as we attempted to interpret each piece. Sometimes we responded by answering questions and often, we were able to express ourselves through art. We became artists using watercolors, pastels, and charcoals. She had us complete a poetry book with all of our favorite writers. We made them in a round circle from assorted construction paper and markers. At the top, we punched two holes and selected ribbon to tie the book together. I gave my daisy decorated poetry book to my father and he still has it today.

One entire wall at South Street School was small paned windows where I could escape with every story read to me. I loved it when it snowed during winter school days. I would get lost listening to Ms. Zucca's stories and watching the tiny white pedals flutter down from the sky. Was I really listening to the stories and paying attention or was I lost in my own stories yet to be told? She made each of us dreamers and allowed us the freedom of discovery.

As winter melted away into spring, our summer days were nearing. The summer meant Cape Cod, fried clams, and picking periwinkles along the rocky cove landscape. It also meant missing Ms. Zucca. I knew she loved seashells and always during our summer trips to the cottage at Buzzards Bay, I would search for the prettiest seashells to collect for her.

I would bring my red plastic pail and while bent over like a crooked crab, I would hand select the smoothest and prettiest seashells. It was a pleasant and peaceful hunt, only the echoes of small motorboats revving their engines as they headed out of the bay against the tide. The seagulls diving for their daily fish would screech as they dove into the choppy waters. My search was on as I, too, became a scavenger of the sea, harmoniously one with nature, asking nothing except for it's remaining beauty.

There were loads of mussel shells, and halves of soft clam shells. These shells were brilliant white. Ridged white and gray cohoug shells were like polka dots lining the white foamy coastline. I continued to pick, sort, and dip each shell into the salty waters for cleaning and acceptance. These would be so beautiful to send to Ms. Zucca, I pondered, thinking of The Family under the Bridge *story. The seashells were my friends, my "friends under the bridge," and the beauty Ms. Zucca had taught me to accept and to give back.*

With my red pail, I shuffled through the sand and occasionally stopped to pick up another friend. I didn't want to miss a beauty! As I approached the haphazardly formed sea wall around our cottage, I carefully positioned my beautiful seashells in the sun to dry. I made two piles: one for Ms. Zucca; the other for me to keep.

I ran inside the screen door to ask my mom for a small box for Ms. Zucca's seashells. She searched in the kitchen cupboard and located a small brown box with a lid. Perfect!

Later that evening, I softly placed white tissues in the bottom of the box. I thought of my new seashells as tiny pillows on top of the wall outside under the stars of the Cape, glistening white backs reflecting off the moon's glow. I fell asleep thinking about sending my seashells to my favorite teacher.

I woke up to the sounds of the motor boats and fishermen talking at the gate behind the back door to my window. "My seashells..." I thought as I made a mad-dash out the screen door with my little brown box. There they were, my masterpieces of nature. I bent over and placed Ms. Zucca's shells in their new home and darted indoors for a marking pen and tape. Her address was in my Literature folder which I always took with me, especially over long family trips. I never wanted to be without paper and pencil.

"Oh, no," I thought. I have to write a note to her. I'll just keep it simple and direct. "I miss you <u>so much</u>!" I underlined so much for emphasis. Inside, I carefully folded the note in half and

topped my shore friends with one more tissue. Finally, I taped the sides of the box and addressed the label. I placed the box on the kitchen table for my mom to mail out the next day.

The box was sent to Danbury to the person who had always made stories come alive for me. I hope the seashells made it safely. Moreover, I hope she really knew how much I missed her. I missed her stories and getting lost in them. Ms. Zucca had taught me discovery and the little joys in life. Each day in class with her, she gave me the freedom to dream. Each day without her, I teach others how to dream without me.

Chapter 5

THE NOSE BLEED

It was sixth period and such a glorious day. I thought it would be enjoyable for students to go outside behind the portable and read. First, I took attendance and instructed my students to take the literature books from the desks and bring their backpacks as well. The students formed two straight lines and off we headed to the football field surrounded by soft green grass and warm sunshine. They never liked holding hands to form a large circle, but somehow they always joined in.

The students formed a large egg shape next to each other and sat down. Often, many of the students propped up their backpacks and created a stiff "lounge" to read in a comfortable position. The students selected "popcorn" as their reading strategy for the final period of the day. When students read, they randomly call on another classmate to read after them. If they catch their friend lost or off task, the student has to sit outside of the circle until they locate where we are reading, and they are ready to participate.

It was approaching two forty-five in the afternoon and dismissal was at two-fifty. The students had really enjoyed reading Sandra Cisneros' short story, *Eleven.* After reading and discussing how the character felt in the story, students placed the textbooks in four piles next to me.

I explained that tomorrow in class, they would be completing a character map describing how the young girl felt in the story as the teacher insisted the red sweater was hers. A few students offered to carry the textbooks to the front of the classroom door and leave them for me to take in after school was over. They returned just as the dismissal announcements were being made.

First, the bike riders and car riders were called, followed by specific bus numbers. We had to really listen for the bus numbers as we were outside and didn't have the visual aid of the television to assist us over the chatter of students who were excited that school was over for the day. I was down to four students waiting for their busses; two for bus 27 and two for bus 19. By now, the five of us were standing and bus 19 was called.

Just as the girls said goodbye to me, Jonathan took his backpack and was tossing it as if it were a large football. I instructed the boys to stop playing around and to listen for their bus number. Right then, Jonathan tossed his back-pack one more time and it landed in his friend's face. The backpack, which was packed with binders, books, and gym clothes landed right into the face of Aaron. As the backpack dropped to the grass, Aaron's nose was now a fountain of blood.

My eyebrows lifted and I yelled over to Jonathan, "Oh my goodness...look what's happened...I told you guys to settle down!" Right after my final word, bus 27 was called and Jonathan declares he's leaving.

I said, "You're not leaving right now...go to Mr. DeVries' room and tell him to call the nurse...we need a cart immediately!"

What Jonathan didn't know about his friend, Aaron, was that he was listed on the Nurse's chart as a "bleeder" and if by chance, he started to bleed, he needed prompt medical attention. Even though we had all of our belongings outside for the literature lesson and class dismissal, I neglected to bring the emergency kit outside with us. I didn't have any gloves, any tissues, no band-aids, nothing. I ran over to Aaron, applied pressure to the bridge of his nose, and waited for the nurses to arrive. Mr. Devries walked out to assist me. Aaron's shirt was now turning red from the amount of blood flooding from his nose. Mr. Devries asked what happened and I explained that the boys were playing around with the backpacks.

The nurse's cart zoomed up and loaded both students. I walked over to my portable, took the textbooks in, and met them in the main office. The nurse had Jonathan fill out a witness statement as she proceeded to get the bleeding under control. Next, she asked me if I was wearing protective gloves.

I replied, "No...I left my emergency kit inside the classroom."

She explained to me that if I had any open cuts on my hands, it was advisable that I go to the district's doctor and if I had come in contact with the blood, I may need a series of Hepatitis shots.

It was nearing four o'clock in the afternoon and both parents were on their way from work to pick up their children. I was so upset that Aaron had been injured simply by playing around with Jonathan. I was thankful that they were both friends and there was no malicious intent with the backpacks. Both families knew each other and the kids played after school together and on weekends. After seeing the parents, I had the afternoon planned out for me to go to the district doctor's office.

I arrived at the doctor's office and was informed that because I had a few little open nicks on my hands from gardening, it was advisable to get the series of Hepatitis shots. At the lower base of my back, I received the shots. Over the next sixth months, I returned three times to complete the series.

I learned a great lesson myself that afternoon when teaching outside of the classroom. Always, and in every circumstance, whether it's to walk to the library or take students to the computer lab, remember to take the emergency kit and gloves wherever we go.

After a decade of teaching, I now have three emergency kits placed around the classroom. One by the front door, one by the television, and one in my teacher desk draw. Sometimes the students think I'm a worry wart.

"Let's take the emergency kit with us, better safe than sorry." And off we go, prepared for the unknown.

Chapter 6

THEODORE TAYLOR

Around my classroom are framed treasures of students on memorable field trips, dressed as famous Egyptians for our activity days, and pictures of special people in my life. I have always shared my photographs of my mom, sister, niece and nephews on the second day of school during a lesson called, "Getting to know you." I think it's important for students to connect with their teacher from the start and know a little bit about their history and family.

Each year, the students ask me about several photographs ornately framed and displayed. "Is that your father?" They would ask as the framed photos passed from student to student.

"No, that's a very special author. His name is Mr. Taylor and in the past, he would visit my students in Oceanside and talk with my classes about writing his book, "The Cay."

My friendship with Mr. Taylor started over the summer of 1994. I had just been asked to open Orange Groves Middle as a sixth grade CORE teacher, teaching two blocks of Language Arts and Social Studies classes. I had received the reading requirement list of novels and <u>*The Cay*</u> *was one of them.*

During my leisure time, which was often spent by the pool, I began reading his novel. By the time I reached chapter fifteen, I had tears rolling down my cheeks in the heat of the sun. "Who could possibly write a book and have the main character die?" I thought to myself, as I was nearly out of breath.

I gathered my towel and beach bag and headed towards my apartment. I reached for the telephone, dialed information and asked for the number for Theodore Taylor in any city in California. I received three phone numbers, one of them was from Laguna Beach. I dialed it nervously and at the other end heard a gruff, "Hello..." I stated my name and asked if this was the author of the book, <u>*The Cay*</u>*?*

Mr. Taylor informed me that indeed, he was the one. I explained that I was a newly hired teacher in Oceanside and that I was in the process of reading his book, as it was required reading for my students. I explained that I was so surprised to read Timothy had died in a fierce tempest in chapter fifteen.

Mr. Taylor shared, "Yes, I had to make a profound climax in order for my message to be effec-

tive."

I said it had definitely affected me. The theme of survival between an eleven year old blind Caucasian boy stranded with a seventy year old West Indian on an island after a hurricane needed an intense moment like this. Moreover, the profound theme of prejudice and its effects are the basis for writing The Cay.

That day was the start of over a decade of correspondence, sharing ideas, and visits from Mr. Taylor to my classroom.

Each year, I would send Mr. Taylor a list of student names and he would forward an autographed brochure to each student. The pamphlet included a mini-autobiography along with an overview of the writing process for his book, The Cay. He always signed, "The Best, Theodore Taylor," and indeed he was.

Little did I know from that first anxious phone call that this relationship would develop over the years. He has been such an inspiration to me as a teacher and as a writer. Mr. Taylor, as I referred to him, although he always invited me to call him Ted, knew my passion for teaching. He knew I also wanted to write, but I would always share that I was still gathering my life experiences to put down into a book. Often, during our phone conversations, I would exchange an idea, perhaps about a little boy stranded during a war and left to survive with an enemy on a desolate desert.

He would say, "sounds good...write it down," and I would ponder the characters and most intense moment of my story. After all, Mr. Taylor shared with me that he himself was "still learning the three C's of good storytelling: character, conflict, and construction."

To this day, I have every note, every letter with letterhead, every book release from the publisher, and every Christmas card exchanged over the years.

One year, Mr. Taylor was quite upset over a publisher changing the cover of The Cay to some striking orange and black Halloween colors that portrayed the characters as mean and scary. He was enraged at this "awful art" and he asked my students to write directly to the publisher asking the company to reconsider publishing any additional novels with this mistake.

Each student responded to his request and I mailed the letters to the publisher. My students, along with many students around the country, stopped further publications of this unfit jacket.

I am extremely proud of the fact that Mr. Taylor visited Orange Groves Middle School and students were afforded the opportunity to meet a real author. I felt it was valuable for my students to meet an author and ask their own questions, because many of them were future writers. We took photographs and the students were amazed to learn that Mr. Taylor had written the first draft of The Cay in only three weeks! As he explained, "The Cay nearly wrote itself..."

In 2000, I was deeply saddened when I learned that Mr. Taylor had undergone heart surgery. Orange Groves Middle School sent a basket of green plants along with a Get Well balloon. I stayed in touch during his recovery and he reassured me that he was improving each day. Mr. Taylor said that he had a workout regime along with physical therapy and was experiencing a slow, but continual improvement.

I sent out another student list from my Intensive Reading class on September 27, 2006. We had just finished reading The Cay. One month passed...two months passed and I had not received his autographed brochures. I even expressed my concern to my mother and she said, "Well, Deb, you have to call him."

I called the phone number I had connected to

Mr. Taylor with over the years. The outgoing message was, "The number was no longer in service; please check the number you have dialed."

The next day, another teacher friend and I were driving to a baby shower for a colleague. While driving, she asked me a question that completely startled me.

"Didn't you hear, Deb, Mr. Taylor died in November. The news is posted on his website."

I took a big gulp as my eyes welled up and as we approached the stop sign, I felt as if my heart had dropped. I was stunned. I hadn't heard and no one had contacted me. I had just lost perhaps the most influential friend and resource as a teacher over the years. He was an inspiration to me, as well as to my students.

Today, I sit with my portfolio collection of dried sea grape leaves and all of our pictures and correspondence over the years. What an inspiration. Mr. Taylor, I know you're watching over me with every strike of letter and typed word.

Finally, my first book! As I begin my journey, I know The Cay will live on forever. Excelsior! Excelsior! Mr. Taylor...

Chapter 7

CHOCOLATE SOUP

Thomas was quite a unique student, some would call him odd. However, I had the opportunity to have Thomas in my Period Four Language Arts class for a year and I understood him. My instruction with Thomas started out a bit rough. I was in contact with his dad because there was an issue of Thomas not completing his homework on a regular basis. Thomas' father and I corresponded back and forth regarding Thomas' agenda, his vocabulary work and reading logs. Finally, Thomas began writing a journal each day in class and like magic, the doors opened. We both smiled and laughed, and our connection creating a positive, enthusiastic learning environment took place.

The day after Halloween, the students entered the classroom, filled out their agendas, received a sticker, and began their journal writing with a quote and response. Following this, the students engaged in "Free Write" where they kept a journal of what *they* wanted to write. After writing, the students volunteered to share with classmates their daily entries.

Thomas energetically raised his hand and

shared that he had received four hundred thirty-two pieces of candy last night trick-or-treating with his brother. The students and I were amazed at this amount.

Tom continued, "If you figure that there are fifty-five days until Christmas Day, that works out to about eight pieces of candy that I could eat each day without running out." Thomas' eyes were wide, sporting a huge smile as he went on, "That doesn't include the little candy treats, like from gas stations, and from stores that my mom buys me."

I had no words, only the biggest, genuine smile on my face, as did the rest of the students. Thomas was a character alright. He always reminded me of Sam, one of the characters in the book series, *Time Warp Trio* by Jon Scieska.

Tom was always calculating and figuring out something that the ordinary person would overlook. He had the brains and took the time to find the end result. Perhaps that's why Tom was in Honors Math class.

The students and I followed Thomas' progress with his single allotment of only 7.8 pieces of candy per day until Christmas. Of course, he shared, "If I fudge here or there, and eat an extra two pieces one night, I'll just cut back the following night by two pieces and then it'll balance out."

We could only laugh with his genuineness and mathematical skills regarding his wealth of candy. To be sure, Thomas sweetened our days with his stories and his love for chocolate, which in turn, made him a writer of sweets.

After Christmas, students returned and all the boys and girls in Period Four couldn't wait to share their "Free Writes" in their journals. And of course, we were all on the edge of our seats waiting to hear if Thomas had any candy left.

Thomas asked the class, "Have you ever heard of Candy Soup?" As he shared his journal each of us forgot we were in a class and entered the 'Sweet Life of Thomas."

"All you do," he said, as he continued to read his journal with butterscotch eyes and a syrupy smile, "you microwave as many little pieces of chocolate as you can fit in a soup bowl. Next, you microwave it for a minute watching to make sure it doesn't boil over. You take it out and break up little pieces of red licorice and microwave that again, for about 30 seconds. Then take that out and then add several pieces of those little red and white mints, about six is good, and microwave that again for thirty seconds. When it comes out....mmmmm, it is so good and the spearmints really give the chocolate mixture a nice taste."

There wasn't a sound in the room. Students sat in their seats and listened, as if we were at a cinema watching a movie on a big screen and devouring buttery popcorn at the most intense moment in the movie.

"Finally, you take a strand of red licorice, and cut each end off and that becomes your straw. Of course, you do this after the chocolate soup has cooled. Now, you can drink your soup by sucking it through the licorice straw!"

A student sitting by the window raised his hand and asked, "Thomas, can you really suck it though the licorice? Does it really work?"

"Yeah, it really is just like a straw. I guess it would depend on what kind of licorice you bought, though, if the circumference of the interior was large enough, " Thomas offered.

As a teacher, sometimes I really don't know where my students will take the lesson. Most of the time, I have a specific end result. However, with journaling, it's risky business, and this journal sharing was a sweet delight. I asked, "What about your stomach, after eating all of that sugar? Oh my goodness, Tom, were you okay?"

Thomas' eyes almost left his sockets as he added, "Oh yeah, it was worth a little stomach ache. MMMMMMmmm! It was so good! You should try it."

We each had a sweet treat that day with Tom's journal sharing. He became a great writer of expository and creativity. Who knows? Perhaps one day he will be a famous chef making sugary treats around the world. As a teacher, I knew he had developed his skills in writing, reading, and speaking. I knew Thomas had evolved into an engaged and successful student in grade six, now wanting to complete his assignments. A teacher could ask nothing else.

Yes I could! I could ask for one more homemade chocolate recipe and one great quote:

"Even though the worst stomach ache brings you happiness, you must remember...the tasty chocolate lives on forever." ***Thomas***

Chapter 8

DR. BARNES

I started my teaching career at Orange Grove Middle School thinking that I would be the best teacher in the world. I had always grown up with chalkboards and erasers decorating the basement walls in our home. My neighborhood friends would come over to play and I would take charge and begin teaching them at my makeshift classroom. I always "played" teacher; now it was time to be a real teacher.

I now was equipped with the appropriate credentials and training to enter the world of children learning. My first class just needed, "a little extra love," shared my first principal, Dr. Pat Barnes. I was the fourth teacher taking over the classroom of eighth grade Language Arts students at the end of the school year. Somehow, the teacher that was previously hired lacked the certificate for teaching English, and fortunately for me, this became my first class.

As I peeked through the small rectangle framed window on the classroom door, it was like watching the movie, "Dangerous Minds" starring Michelle Phiefer. Students were hanging out against the classroom walls, as well as sit-

ting on top of the tabletops.

Dr. Barnes asked me if I wanted her to introduce me to the students and I replied, "No, thank you, I can handle it."

As I reached for the silver classroom doorknob and began to turn it, I could hear the chanting of students in unison, "We want Mr. Bell, we want Mr. Bell, we want Mr. Bell..."

To this day, I can still hear, "We want Mr. Bell." With my green briefcase draped over my shoulder, I turned the cold knob, entered the room of strange, but youthful faces, and firmly stated, "Come on now, let's take our seats." I swiftly headed for the overhead stand to the attendance sheets. I was directed and I had a mission. I had a curriculum to teach and I needed the students in their seats and ready to learn.

Students were supposed to sit down and learn, that was their job in life; I now had mine. A couple of students actually sat down. I restated my instructions to sit down, and of course, I had a few resistant students who wanted to take their own stand. Finally, to my amazement, I had all students in their seats and took the daily attendance. Students were talking and not paying attention, however, they tolerated my mispronunciations of their names as they corrected me.

I had already prepared their weekly vocabulary for "Diary of Anne Frank." After the attendance was taken, I placed the words on the overhead and instructed the class to take out paper and pencils and begin copying down the vocabulary.

One student shouted out, "Where's Mr. Bell? He was cool...he didn't make us do any work."

Others began to chime in... "We want Mr. Bell!"

I explained that he was now in another classroom and that Dr. Barnes placed me in this classroom to finish out the school year. I scanned the classroom to make sure that everyone had paper and pencils to write down their words. I observed three students without paper and walked over to their desks, smiled as I made eye contact, and placed the blank sheets on top of their desks. One student looked up from her desk and asked me, "How do we know you won't leave us like he did?"

I reassured her and the class that I would finish the school year with them. The message was profound. They thought that I was another substitute that was a "fill-in" and wouldn't make it to the end of the year. They wanted consistency in their lives. They wanted someone who would not go away; they wanted one person by their sides.

With this strong sentiment in my heart, I found myself in a hunch-back position canvassed above the overhead with my black marker. The students and I started to discuss the words and meanings. They shared where they were in the textbook and began to locate the words on specific pages.

Just then, the classroom doorknob turned and in walked Dr. Barnes. She swiftly approached the overhead, looked at me with reassuring eyes, and whispered, "You're doing a fine job." She placed two Hershey kisses on top of the overhead. She walked away and exited the classroom smiling at the class as they worked. This was the first time I realized that I really had classroom management under control.

That was the first of many smiles I received from Dr. Barnes over the next decade of teaching for her. She was my mentor, my support system, my encourager, and she was the one who pushed me further than anyone whom I had ever met. I taught grade six for ten years under her leadership. Dr. Barnes supported me and in-

spired me to go on as Literacy Coach for the district.

With this one year position, I trained teachers to implement effective reading and writing strategies in the classroom. Furthermore, Dr. Barnes wanted me to go on and become a principal. However, after one year of working with adults as a Literacy Coach, I missed the students so much, I wanted to return to the classroom. I did not want to deal with the problems of the school, such as referrals, and all of the responsibilities of running an entire school. I just wanted to teach my students.

I wanted my little classroom back with youthful, wondering minds, and joys of inspiration that make up each day. Dr. Barnes understood. To this day, we stay in contact, even after I moved to Florida and continue to teach sixth grade. We have been through marriages together, divorces, deaths, and births. When I return to San Diego, we try to visit and share each past year filled with stories of life. She will remain my guide of inspiration and one of the individuals who believed in me and supported me over my years of growing as a teacher.

Dr. Barnes taught me the value of connecting with each student and to let the students know that you value them. Once you have made that connection, you will have success with students. I carry that philosophy with me in the classroom today.

Each day, I build meaningful relationships with my students. I actually think this is supported daily through "journal sharing." The students share their responses to a quote on the board and also write a paragraph about their lives. That's when the connections occur as they open up and share their worlds with their classmates.

There will only be one Dr. Barnes. She has made me the teacher I am today and for that I carry on her mission in life; to value each person for who they are. She continues to run a school in California after a brief period of retirement. I know she is continuing to inspire others at her school site because this is her destiny in life and her gift.

To my mentor, my first principal, my friend, I thank you for such wisdom in the teaching profession. More importantly, thank you for believing in me.

Chapter 9

Helen's Smile

There's nothing like hearing your name called across campus at seven-thirty in the morning requesting you to report to the principal's office. I was in my classroom changing the date on the whiteboard and jumped. I picked up my keys, reached for paper and pencil, locked the door and headed to the principal's office.

"Mrs. Burggraaf, please report to the front office." I couldn't walk fast enough. As I trudged to the top of the tiered main campus, I reflected over my morning meetings. I was sure that I was clear this morning. What could this possibly be about, I thought, as I passed by the seventh grade wing and waved good morning to Dr. Woods. I entered the Administration Building to find the principal's door closed. Her door was always open. She was available to see you at any time and welcomed teachers and students with open arms. However this morning, I faced a cold, brown door and began to feel unsure of what I was about to encounter.

As quickly as I knocked, the door opened and I was greeted with forced smiles wrapped around serious looks of sadness. I was asked to sit down and began introductions.

The principal asked, “Mrs. Burggraaf, you have Helen in one of your classes?”

“Yes, I do, in period three,” I confirmed.

“Well, this is Helen’s neighbor, Mrs. Goodaul, she lives across the street from Helen’s family.”

I shook her hand with a smile to match the room.

My principal continued with introductions. “These two young ladies are Helen’s friends and Mrs. Goodaul’s daughters, Sarah and Lacey.”

“Good morning, nice to meet you,” I stated, trying to guess the ages of the daughters. I thought both of them were fourth or fifth grade students and I wondered why they were at Orange Grove Middle this morning. They should be in school.

“Mrs. Burggraaf,” the principal continued, “Helen is in the nurse’s office right now. Mrs. Goodaul is here at Orange Grove to report suspected child abuse. Helen was over at her house this morning and they brought her in. The authorities have been called and Helen is with the nurses now in the clinic.”

My mind raced at seven forty-five in the morning. Abuse. What kind of abuse? Helen was a big, tall girl from a large family from Samoa. She always wore a slanted smile across her face and didn't speak very much, even when working in group or on a collaborative class project. Helen was quiet, too quiet. I wanted her to talk more, to socialize more, to interact with her peers more. "What could have possibly happened?" Thoughts were racing through my mind.

Smiles were now erased from our faces. I looked at my principal with stark eyes and a dropped heart and asked, "What kind of abuse? Is she alright?"

The principal leaned forward as she always did and placed her elbows on her knees with her head as close to you as she could possibly bend towards you and said, "Helen has a questionable mark on the inside of her leg that needed to be reported."

My eyes welled with water and a melon took over my throat. I couldn't be professional now. I couldn't believe what I was hearing. A mark on her leg! How did the mark get there? What type of mark was this on a young girl now sitting in the Nurse's office?

It was eight o'clock now and the first period bell rang. Thirteen hundred students were now mobile and making their way across campus to their first period classes. The principal reached out her hand to me and said, "Mrs. Burggraaf, I'll keep you posted during the day as to how Helen is doing.

"Of course." I swallowed hard just to get the words out. Now I'm supposed to walk down to my classroom and teach my literature lesson? I was a mess. Tears draped down my face and I could feel an instant blossoming of a cold sore from the stress.

"How could anyone do this to *my* Helen?" She became mine. She was not the daughter of someone else's family; she was mine and I was angered. I wanted to be with her but couldn't. I had a hundred students to teach today and there she sat in the nurse's office with strangers, feeling lost.

I forced my warm smile to students and said, "Good morning." It was far from a good morning for me. I felt like a ghost teacher walking to my classroom. I was envisioning what the mark looked like and how *anyone* could do this to a child. My students were lined up at the front door, talking and full of energy, waiting to get into the classroom and start their day.

The announcements began over the PA system, followed by the pledge of allegiance and attendance. This morning became ritual without feeling. I made it through the day teaching Jose Jimenez's, "The Circuit." It is a short story about a young boy in school and how it feels to be raised in a family of migrant workers always mobile, packing up, and looking for work.

My lip felt like it was the size of a small golf ball. At lunch, I first went to see Dr. Grady, a grade six counselor because I was so upset. This was not my first suspected child abuse, but it didn't matter. They all feel like the first when they happen. You feel sick to your stomach and it doesn't go away. Dr. Grady shared that now that Child Protective Services were involved, they would handle the investigation.

"It will be okay, Mrs. Burggraaf." She stood up and gave me a warm hug and I could see the care in her eyes. It didn't feel okay.

"This will never be okay," I thought to myself.

The rest of the day was rote teaching. I tried to have enthusiastic emotion and excitement, but I was drained. I was drained from not being able to help Helen and I was drained from not getting more involved. I knew Helen was quiet, but I thought to myself, what was she holding in? Did she have anyone she could talk to? How long was this going on?

At two-fifty in the afternoon, the dismissal bell rang and I was empty. It was time to go home and I felt nothing. Where was Helen? What would happen next? Who would she stay with? Where would she go? All I knew was that I didn't want her to return to her family and I wanted her safe and cared for.

One week later, Helen returned to the classroom with her familiar slanted smile and tall, quiet walk. We smiled at each other and I offered a warm heart open for her to accept. Helen was herself the rest of the school year. She never really talked very much or opened up to her peers. She remained within herself, not really sharing with anyone. Near the end of the school year, I remember she told me that she had moved in with her aunt, her dad's sister. A sigh of relief brushed over me as I felt perhaps this was a safer environment for her.

Students pass through your classes and come and go. Many students come back the next year to visit or simply stop by, wave and yell, "Hi, Mrs. Burggraaf!"

I never saw Helen again, yet she remains in my heart today. I can only hope she is now safe from the world she once was part of. I thought teaching was simply teaching, however, it's so much more than that. It's meetings, and planning, it's 504s and IEPs (Individual Educational Plans), it's evaluations and assessments, it's bus duty and grading papers, and sadly, it's reporting suspected child abuse.

To me, reporting suspected child abuse is the least favorite part of my career. Yet, I am thankful for an institution that protects our children. Our students need us, not only to teach them, but to protect them. Today, Helen is now an adult. I hope she is lively, full of hope, and knows happiness in her life. I hope her marks from the past are erased and she wears a big, genuine smile filled with joy.

Chapter 10

FIELD TRIPS

Bob DeVries had been my partner for over eight years at Orange Grove Middle. We shared the same group of students. I taught them Language Arts and Social Studies; Bob taught Mathematics and Science. After our first couple of years together, we really had developed the "team teaching" concept. Because we shared the same planning period, Bob and I could work on the curriculum and take advantage of the opportunity to discuss the successes, as well as concerns of specific students.

Bob and I felt it was very important to reward our students with several outings. We would plan field trips every six weeks for our students at the end of each grading period.

Field trips were a great incentive for our students as they encouraged students to complete their assignments and turn them in on time. Our field trips were like clockwork. Because of the personal contacts we made over the years, we were able to successfully conduct field trips for sixty students each year.

First, we would tour the newspaper facility

and then walk down to the Pacific Ocean for an afternoon lunch. The students enjoyed playing basketball, running around in Buccaneer Park, or strolling along the ocean, where they would chase the waves and then wait for the rebound of salt water to attack them. Many of the students and I would search for the perfect seashell or sand dollar. I remember students always asking how far they could go into the ocean. Bob and I would always reply, "up to your knees."

Every year, we would have students that would look like drenched kids hit by a tidal wave. We would have them sit along the huge coastal rocks to dry off. We told them, "Okay, now you're ROCKED!!!"

Another field trip we would make in the fall was to a local museum in Balboa Park to view the mummies. Nothing excited the students more than to see an Egyptian sarcophagus. The students were divided into teams of thirty with a teacher, three or more parents, and a docent from the museum. This trek was so wonderful as it tied perfectly into the sixth grade Social Studies curriculum, which included the study of Ancient Egypt.

Our students had learned about the mummification process, canopic jars, and famous kings and pharaohs. I was so proud of my students when they were able to answer the docent's questions while on tour of the museum.

For example, "How old was King Tutankhamen when he died? How did the Egyptians prepare the body for the afterlife? What is the Ba and Ka and why was this important to the Egyptians?" They really had learned about the ancient Egyptians and I gleamed like a proud parent.

Our next planned field trip was to a sea aquarium in La Jolla, California. Here, the focus was on science and mathematics. At this museum, students were able to experience "hands-on" activities that had meaning to them. Students touched prickly star fish and felt slimy sea cucumbers. They observed the power of the earth's magnetic pull by seeing wave motion in action. Finally, students enjoyed a picnic lunch at tables provided outside of the facility. Students would share their sandwiches and cookies. The big event of the day was to go to the snack bar and buy ice cream and sodas. Souvenirs were expensive so many times I would buy the students bookmarks or pencils.

A field trip that cost us nothing but planning, was walking down the hill for our annual visit to a well known book store. Each year, this book store provided our students with a free tour. During our excursion, our students were divided into groups of ten, with a teacher and parents. Students were shown books by topic; adventure, mystery, science fiction, drama, crafting, and sports. Specific authors and their locations were identified followed by a read aloud of a picture book from the children's section.

A terrific feature of this tour is that this book store offers a summer reading program to encourage students to continue to read over the summer. Bob and I would try and make this our final field trip specifically for this reason. With this program, after reading three books and keeping a "reading log," parents sign off on a sheet confirming that their child did read each book. The students return the completed reading log to the book store and they receive a free reading book that is valued at five dollars or less. Often, parents are so busy working and they just don't have enough time to take their children to a bookstore. A single visit to the bookstore and enrollment in the summer reading program encourages families to read more.

Today, Bob and I talk often about our field trips with the students and how much fun we had. We are now limited to one field trip per year and it must be curriculum related. Additionally, all parents and school volunteers must be fingerprinted and cleared by a security check at the School District.

For example, at Limestone Middle School, our field trip this year was to a local museum. Students were very excited to attend this trip. However, in order to qualify, each student had to obtain a certain amount of points from a Reading Program before they could participate in the end-of-the year field trip.

Students get excited about leaving campus and going out into the "real world," which is what I enjoyed most. The trips gave our students the opportunity to not only become book smart in school, but to observe something outside of the classroom they might like to pursue on their own after experiencing the field trip.

We had a lot of fun together on our treks around San Diego County. On our final field trip as we were returning to school, we passed a Dollar store. I looked over at Bob and pleaded to take several students in, "just for a minute!" Of course, he said, yes. Twenty minutes later, the students and I exited with numerous bags, full of goodies.

That was over ten years ago and it seems like only last year. Mr. DeVries and I had a tremendously successful team effort together over the years. Each day as partners, we worked together to design a curriculum that was effective and meaningful for all learners. We never went to each other's houses or met for dinner over the years. Yet each day as team teachers, we worked together to design a curriculum that was effective and meaningful for all learners.

Since I started my career teaching in Florida, I have incorporated effective team teaching strategies with my new partner, utilizing much of what I learned working with Bob.

I will never forget Mr. DeVries and his soft demeanor with the students combined with his "sure-we-can" attitude. Anything is possible if you have a positive attitude and are willing to venture out. That's exactly what Bob and I did for our students. We ventured outside of the classroom to the real world they will one day be a part of and manage for themselves.

Chapter 11

KATRINA

It was that time of year again when hormones were racing and keeping students engaged in meaningful activities was challenging. As November approaches, students are getting tired of school and looking forward to the Thanksgiving break. It is a challenging time of the year for teachers and the goal is to keep the students on task and learning. I thought of showing an educational video, however, it was too early in the school year to begin this as a reward.

I have nothing against movies, as I am an avid movie go'er myself. In fact, after state testing, my classes enjoy, "Fun Fridays." This is when I show a movie every two weeks with a special food treat that connects to a specific culture or piece of literature. For example, tasty treats could include an assortment of cookies from around the world. Additionally, I like to include more art activities as the school year progresses based around diverse cultures.

Often as a teacher, we do not have enough time to engage in art because we are required to adhere to the standards that are mandated by the state for each grade level curriculum.

My first period class was an English Language Development class. I was assigned a group of students who spoke Spanish with different learning levels. They were an exciting class to start the morning with at Orange Grove Middle.

Often, mothers would walk their children up to my portable door with a smiling baby in the stroller wrapped in bundles of hand-crocheted pink and blue baby blankets. The parents cherished their children's education, something which many of them lacked. To show their appreciation, I would receive homemade tamales wrapped in crinkled foil for my lunch. I especially enjoyed the sweet tamales with the raisins and sugar. What a treat! I can still savor their special offering of gratitude.

Many of my students in this class lived in one bedroom rented apartments with several brothers and sisters. They lived simple lives. The padre (father) would work long hard days and the mother would stay at home and tend to the baby and toddlers while cooking for the family and maintaining their homes. I had one young girl, Katrina, who was in this class, and told me about the chores she would have to do before she started on her own homework each evening.

Katrina would go home and help her mother finish up the prepared meal for the evening. Next, she would lend a hand folding the clothes, set the table for dinner, and then help her younger sister in grade three with her homework. Her younger brother in grade one would go out behind the apartment and play with his friends in the gravel stone driveway. Kari, as she was called, sat at a small chipped and tattered oval wooden table and helped her sister with her homework.

One of her mother's greatest joys was a large, healthy green plant that emerged from a medium Mexican red clay pot. This green leafy plant traversed around the ceiling of the living room like a wild roller coaster with no design. I've never seen an agapanthus more green with huge leaves as this one. Kari was so very proud of her mother's green thumb and shared this beauty with me one afternoon.

After the family sat together around a small round table adorned with an off white crocheted tablecloth, the girls would clean up the kitchen while her younger brother bathed and started his homework. They had one small black and white television with rabbit ears and Dad sat down with his cervesa to watch the news in Spanish. Kari got her brother going on his homework and darted into the kitchen to help prepare the family's lunch for the following day.

Katrina did not begin her homework or attend to her own needs until after eight in the evening. She made sure that her family was taken care of first; this was the way her family had raised her. She was the eldest and seemed to welcome the tasks at hand each afternoon. She did them well and had her responsibilities down to a science.

This mastery of tasks continued in the classroom. Kari approached me before class one morning to discuss an upcoming lesson. *El Dia de Los Muertos*, or Day of the Dead, was approaching and she thought it would be fun for the students to make some of the decorations in honor of loved ones who had passed on.

November 1, *All Saints Day*, and November 2, *All Souls Day* were only a week away. Kari shared that these were special days honoring both children and adults who have died.

Colorful decorations and family gatherings

are part of this two day celebration. She had the idea to construct a small altar for, "The Day of the Dead," which connected to the student's cultural background. Even though this festivity is connected to death, it is not a dismal or gloomy time. It is a time of happiness, family, fun, food and lots of color. I agreed that this was a fantastic idea and asked her which lesson would she like to teach that would be fun for the students.

Katrina thought that making paper doilies, or "papeles picados," to decorate the offering altar would be a great art activity for the students. This lesson would be easy and not cost too much money for supplies; only tissue paper and scissors. I welcomed the idea and asked if she could provide me with a couple of samples to model for her classmates. Kari was so excited. I gave her several sheets of tissue paper and she went home to plan our lesson.

The next morning, Kari knocked on the portable door before the first bell rang. As she always did, she walked in with her warm smile, long curled brown hair pulled back in a tight ponytail. She shared that she had practiced making the papeles picados last night. Kari placed her large three-ring white binder down and clicked open the metal rings. She proudly took out beautiful masterpieces of intricately cut lace, made from simple tissue paper. I had never seen anything more beautiful. They must have taken her hours, I thought.

When did she have this kind of time? She shared that her mother had helped her and it was really not that hard. Kari was willing to teach my classes how to create these delicate and beautiful wonders for our Dia de Los Muertos altar.

I wrote up the lesson plan and Kari expressed the need for three helpers: Alma, Jasmine, and José. I blocked out two, fifty-five minute periods for this cultural art lesson and the students were excited about next Thursday and Friday.

Kari stood in front of the class with confidence, knowledge, and skill. She offered her classmates step-by-step instructions as she modeled the process of making Mexican doilies.

The class began this activity with zest and created the most beautiful lace, worthy of any Italian lace boutique. Katrina had the ability to direct and lead. She fully embraced her culture and she was ready and willing to share it with others.

Our altar was decorated with beautiful paper lace squares. Even the wall behind our altar was adorned with squares that became a huge patchwork paper quilt. Additionally, students brought in white and black skulls, fruit plates with grapes and apples, clothes that a loved one would wear in the afterlife, and important personal items that were allowed at school—an empty wallet, a small framed photo of a grandfather, packaged tortillas and hot, spicy salsa. These were, "ofrendas" or "offerings," displayed on the most beautiful altar for this special cultural event.

Most importantly, a very special student had her moment to shine as she shared her knowledge with others. The pink, orange, yellow, green, and purple lace decorated the altar and warmed our hearts, as well as those loved ones in another place and time.

Kari continued her success after her year in grade six. She accepted a "Writer of the Year Award" at the end of eighth grade and received five thousand dollars for her essay. Her story was about her parents' struggle to make it to the United States for a better life. Her father made her put all the money into an account and leave it there. By the end of her eighth grade school year, she was working at an indoor swap meet booth selling baby clothes.

Since moving to Florida, Kari and I continue to correspond. She is a successful student attending a prominent University, majoring in Business Mathematics. Katrina is such a well rounded individual in all subjects; she will go far at whatever she attempts in life. Each Christmas, I look forward to receiving her holiday card and an update of her life.

I know she will have two homes one day; one here in the United States and one in Mexico. Kari loves the lifestyle in Mexico and the closeness of walking down the streets, gathering in the tiled Plaza in the center of the village, and greeting everyone with a familiar smile. She will probably work in the United States and raise her family where her parents once started. What a great opportunity for such a young individual with direction, motivation, and the drive to pursue.

Each year, I return to my classroom and open my boxes to set up my room. My heart is always reborn again when I take out a few of Kari's lace doilies that she made. It fills my senses at the start of my year with the thought that *every* individual who walks through those doors has a skill, has value, and will be successful.

My time with Kari as my student was brief. Teachers have one hundred and ninety-six days to inspire. In this case, Kari inspired others and all of us who were touched by her presence are better people and enriched by Kari's joy after being part of *her* life.

Chapter 12

MR. WENZEL

"Kids say and do the darndest things" is a famous quote coined by someone who must have had at least three children. As a teacher, I often think my students are much older in their everyday thinking skills. I teach eleven year olds going on twenty. They are quite book smart and I often find myself wondering if the curriculum is actually for first year high school.

For example, if a box needs a piece of tape placed over it, they struggle. One student actually ripped a four inch strip and placed it vertically over the flaps and thought that was adequate for storage in our cabinet. Of course, I encouraged the student by telling him that what he did was good. However, I modeled the correct way by placing two strips horizontally to match those lengthwise. This would insure fewer bugs invading our paperback novels during the summer months.

"Oh, yeah, that's a great idea, Mrs. Burgraaff," he shared after watching me place the two foot strip of masking tape covering both flaps.

I guess knowing how to function in life is a growing process that takes place over time. Students must also learn this at home. My hat's off to parents because I think this is the most giving and unconditional dedication of love that life has to offer one to another.

I remember driving with my family and sitting in the back seat of my dad's station wagon watching the clouds and sunlight blanket each other and teasing my face as we drove on a Sunday afternoon together. I always had my window cracked to feel the warm afternoon breeze, but more importantly, my parents had smoked in the car and I hated the smell of cigarette smoke wafting to the back seat. I remember getting headaches from the smell of burning tobacco and I would fuss and start a family feud.

"I can't stand it!" I would insist and roll my window down a little further. My sister was by my side and sat there saying nothing, except to nudge me or bicker to start even more of a commotion. Back then, there were no movies or DVDs to watch to keep the children occupied. I remember singing, "One hundred of bottles of beer on the wall, one hundred bottles of beer," or "The wheels on the bus go round and round, round and round..." We must have driven our

parents nuts with the same repetitive songs over and over again.

As much as I disliked the smell of smoke, it didn't stop me from wanting to experiment. As freshmen in high school my friends and I were bored stiff. There were three of us and we were inseparable. One day after school, we contrived the idea that we would each take a couple of cigarettes and matches from our parents and meet at school the next day. We plotted to skip periods four and five because they were after lunch and we really didn't think we would miss much. Additionally, the administrators were still in the lunch room for one of the periods for the later lunches. They were too busy to catch us, so we felt our scheme would go uninterrupted.

Each of them would bring two cigarettes; I would bring along a pack of matches easily found in the junk drawer in the kitchen. We planned to meet out on the football field way out on the furthest set of bleachers. One of my friends had the same period three as me so we would walk together and meet up under the metal seats.

The bell rang signaling the end of period three and my heart raced. "Should I do this? What if I get caught? I don't even like to smoke...

why was I doing this? I'm an 'A' student. Will I get in major trouble?" I remember so many thoughts running through my head, but it was too late to back out now. My friends were counting on me being there.

Off we went like charging race horses set free from the gate. We walked and walked and saw no one, just fields of dry grass and silver metal bleachers ahead of us. We could see our friend just behind us catching up as we approached our little hideaway.

"Did you bring yours, Deb?"

"Yeah, I have the matches," I nervously replied. "Are you sure we won't get caught?" I asked this as my hands shook taking out the matches from my bag.

One friend chimed in, "We're here now, it's too late to go back to class."

With that thought, I struck my first match without success. I thought it was a lot easier; I had watched my parents light up a million times. I tried again as one of my friends cupped her hands around me to guard off the zephyr of wind. Another match was struck and finally, ignition! We kept guard by looking up from under the seats of our hideout and we felt scared, but safe. We knew what we were doing was wrong, but we kept doing it.

I lit my friend's cigarette. As she coughed, choking and trying to clear the smoke away from her face, Mr. Wenzel, the vice-principal magically appeared from nowhere. It was as if he had been dropped from the sky.

"Ladies, stand up and give me the cigarettes, NOW!" He commanded. "Come with me," he ordered and we picked up our backpacks. I remember shaking and starting to cry. I was a nervous wreck.

"What would happen to us now?" I thought as I kept my head down, crying and looking at the crunched up golden grass.

Mr. Wenzel was a small man, almost a mini replica of Vladimir Putin. He was a humble man and I really didn't have much to do with him during the school year, except at assemblies or when he made his entrance into a classroom to observe. He was always well dressed; wore a suit and tie and walked staunch and upright with a firm stride carrying his small frame.

"Sit down," he ordered, as we sat just outside his office. He contacted our parents while we sat.

"Why didn't I think we'd get caught? What a stupid thing to do. I hate smoking!" So many thoughts raced through my head. "What's going to happen next, what will my dad do?

Mr. Wenzel brought each of us into his office as our parents arrived. My father walked in with no face. I sat by his side. Mr. Wenzel informed my father that I was going to receive a referral for this unfortunate event. My dad was quiet; he didn't look at me and I couldn't seem to face him either. My father asked Mr. Wenzel, "How could such a good student mess up so badly?"

"Well, we all make mistakes, sir, sometimes we have to learn the hard way," Mr. Wenzel offered.

We drove home and not a word was said in the car. I don't even remember the ride home. I went to my bedroom and cried and cried. I didn't know what was going to happen next. I remember my dad poking his head in the door saying, "You're grounded for the next two weeks and I don't want you hanging out with those two girls anymore."

I'm not very proud of this event in my life. True, it was a learning experience. It also supports the idea of how my own students today don't think things through all of the time. I didn't and I had a price to pay.

After receiving my teaching credentials in December of 1993, I wanted to return to my high school and see several teachers, and of course, Mr. Wenzel. The day before I was to visit, I phoned the school secretary to inquire about visiting my former English and French teachers and I asked if I could visit Mr. Wenzel in the afternoon.

"Mr. Wenzel?" The school secretary raised her voice. "Haven't you heard? You'd better hurry to the hospital to see him. He's on his last leg and won't last much longer. He's dying, dying from lung cancer...smoked too much over the years."

My heart dropped as I heard this terrible news. Mr. Wenzel had tried to stop me from smoking in years past because he knew smoking was a terrible habit. He tried to protect me from getting started and now his smoking habit was about to cost him his life.

I didn't go to the hospital to see him. I didn't want to see him that way. I wanted him proud of me for becoming a teacher and finally growing up. I wanted to remember him as the humble, "Vladimir Putin," the protector and wise man of students. Amazing to me even until today, the one thing Mr. Wenzel tried to stop me from doing, he died from.

This year, one of my students was quite a challenge for other teachers, but was easy for me. Often, he was on the path of being viewed as a "problem" child. He even had broken into the school during spring break. He cracked a window trying to get in and set off the alarm. When we returned to school, he shared with me that he was bored and just "didn't think."

He was one of the nicest, most polite students I had all year; always willing to help others with kind and thoughtful gestures. I even selected this student to receive the "Most Improved" award at the end of the year. He deserved it as he started to finally think things through before doing them. Sometimes it's not all academic growing up; sometimes it's just the day-to-day life routine the students learn throughout each year.

That's what I try to do with my students. You can't share all stories with them about your life experiences, but you can guide the children in the right direction. I hope I can continue to guide them during the school year as Mr. Wenzel had done with me. There aren't any bad kids out there; just kids who haven't grown up yet and are still making thoughtless decisions. I honor Mr. Wenzel and thank him for his dedication guiding students in the right direction.

Chapter 13

FIRST PIMPLE

I remember greeting my students at the door with positive instructions. "Please take out your agendas and copy your assignments. Take out your spirals and write down and respond to the *Quote for the Day,* and let's make it a great day at Orange Grove Middle!" Following these instructions, I'd swoop my right arm to motion for students to enter and take their seats.

As usual, it seems that every student needs you. One student forgot his identification badge and needs a temporary badge. Another student needs to go to the counselor for a schedule change because he fractured his wrist at basketball practice last night and can no longer take Gym class. Another student needs to turn in a parent note for her absence the previous day, and one student shares that she finished her expository paper last night and asks if I can edit it today. Instantly, I hear, "Mrs. Burggraaf, Joey has a nose bleed," echoed from group two's table.

I run over to the box of Kleenex and give Joey several tissues and send him to the nurse as the Pledge of Allegiance is heard over the intercom. As Joey exits the door, I motion for students to stand as I place my right hand over my heart. "And justice for all."

As the announcements begin, students are busy taking out their agendas and spiral notebooks. I circulate the room making contact with each student, rewarding them with stickers as they write down their assignments. At the same time, I addressed all of the needs I heard as they entered the classroom. Everyone, at least for the moment, is feeling happy.

The "I can handle it" attitude always seems to kick in each morning. I have improved with this juggling act over the years. Instead of having the ability to manipulate three balls, I feel I can handle eight at times. As the students complete their responses to the quote, I have the next task ready and waiting to keep the students from getting bored and acting out due to being off task. Their lesson for the day was weekly vocabulary: fifteen words with synonyms, antonyms, and a "knock-out" sentence. The vocabulary words were projected on the LCD screen for those students who completed their work early.

The students are great at age eleven. They still love going to school and generally love and respect their teachers. They enjoy seeing their friends and eating lunch with them, as well as rotating to different teachers instead of being in the same classroom with the same teacher all day as they did in elementary school.

As the class settled down, I assisted students as needed. We "echo read" aloud the quote. This is a reading strategy where students chime in and repeat the statement read aloud in class. It is a safe reading strategy because if you don't understand a word, it's okay. No one will notice as others are speaking next to you.

Joey returned from the nurse and placed his pass on my desk. One student, Elizabeth raised her hand. As I approached her group, I bent down next to her and asked, "So, how are we doing today, Elizabeth?"

"Mrs. Burggraaf, I think I have a headache," she shared as she rubbed her soft pale, white forehead above her right eye. "It hurts right here," she said, while showing me the troublesome spot. She was now rubbing her forehead as her eyebrows bent into a frown showing her pain.

After glancing at the raised red-pudgy nodule on her forehead, I whispered, "Elizabeth, it seems you have your first pimple. I'll send you to the nurse and she will give you a soothing compress for it. That should make it feel better. You're nearly a teenager now and this is normal. I know it hurts." Elizabeth's eyes widened with excitement, temporarily forgetting her pain.

"I do? I really have a pimple?" Her wide smile showed approval as she forgot her pain for the moment. I got up from her desk and gave her the pass for the nurse.

She gleamed ear to ear walking out of the classroom as if just receiving the "I'm a Teenager-Now Award." The pain seemed to be worth it because she was growing up. Elizabeth had made it; she was indeed becoming a teenager.

As the door to the classroom closed, students were ready to share their responses to the daily quote, "No pain, no gain." Students enthusiastically raised their hands to share.

"I think this means that we all grow up at our own pace and no one can force us to be something we're not." Students snapped it up, clicking their fingers together to show approval.

Joey chimed in, "Yeah, we grow up when we want to in life; sometimes it hurts to grow up," and again the class snapped it up. Several students continued to share and finally, the class was ready to start their lesson for the day.

Spiral notebooks closed and vocabulary workbooks came out. I smiled a warm approval as the students knew exactly what to do next. Yes, the students were all growing up before my eyes each day. The students were right; they grow up at their own pace. Sometimes, however, Mother Nature has her own calling and overrides their young, whimsical approaches to life and demands change. Elizabeth just found this out and seemed to welcome the growth process into adulthood. Her "headache" was a small price to pay.

For Elizabeth, becoming a teenager was worth a little pain as she pressed a small zip-lock baggie of ice over her eyebrow. I caught a smile from her across the room. Her face said it all; her pain was worth her gain.

Chapter 14

THE KEY SHOP

I had always looked forward to going to work with my dad. My parents owned two bicycle and locksmith shops in Connecticut. I would get dropped off after school in front of the store in Danbury. I looked forward to playing with the money in the cash register and making simple house keys for customers. I even went to work with my father on Saturday mornings.

Saturdays were always great days as I would start my mornings with a Coke and glazed donut from the Five and Dime Shop across Main Street. It was a little store with circular, red swivel seats. I loved sitting there watching the girls fill delicious orders while waiting for my Saturday morning treat! I would return to the key shop and fill my vessels with sugar for the day and start brushing off the brass shavings from the key machines with little paint brushes.

At lunchtime, I carefully crossed the four lane street again for a hotdog with sauerkraut and another Coke. I sure enjoyed the tasty benefits when I worked with my dad. I loved to look in the store at the barrettes and handkerchiefs, the little wallets and makeup purses. When my order was filled, I crossed the street again with my Styrofoam cup slushing with cubed ice and cold soda.

Often, the customers really didn't want to be waited on by an eleven year old girl, especially when it pertained to their keys. Many times, customers questioned my dad if their keys would work when they got home. He always reassured them that if there was a problem, to return the keys and he would correct it.

Maybe they didn't want me to make their keys but they would let me take their money. One day, an older gentleman opened the palm of his hand and after I rang him up, I placed his change in his aged, white palm.

"Young lady," he offered, "you need to be able to count back the change in case the amount you entered into the register is incorrect."

My eyes welled and I felt a lump in my throat. I didn't know how to "count back change." I only knew to give back the amount shown on the cash register.

"Here, let me show you." He began to count back his change from a twenty dollar bill. As he

counted out loud, I wasn't listening. I didn't know how to do this. My dad hadn't shown me. I was frustrated and upset.

Just then, my father approached from behind the work counter where the bicycles were placed for repairs and stood beside me. "This is a good lesson for you to learn, Deb. It takes time to know how to handle money. Thank you, sir," he shared.

With this, the customer insisted that I try to count back the change. I attempted this mathematical task very slowly. I discovered that once the change was counted back to five dollars, then making it to twenty dollars was easy. The old man smiled at me and as he left the front door of the bike shop, he waved and said, "Keep practicing, you'll get better at it."

He was right. I did get better at counting back money and I was quite proud of myself for having the ability to do so. I'd even watch people in other stores to see if they could count back change, and more times than not, they could not. They would just hand over the money and the transaction was a closed deal.

I loved my time with my dad. I remember getting up before him in order to get ready for work. *Dad drove an old blue and white Volkswagen van with the name of his locksmith shop on each side. One particular early Saturday morning, I opened the passenger side of the dewed bus and hopped in and closed the door. My dad was right behind me with the back end of the hatch window opened in the rear. I knew he had to load up items for work each Saturday. As I waited, I began to get antsy.*

"Come on, Dad, let's go, it's already past eight-thirty."

"I'm almost ready, honey," he shared from across the rows of brass key blanks, key machines and back seat. Just then, his voice changed, and firmly ordered, "Deb, get out of the van Now!"

"What?" I looked back at him and questioned his sensibility. "Dad, we've got to go, come on!"

"Deb," he continued in a deeper and stricter tone, "Get out of the van NOW!"

I thought to myself, well, there could be a bee inside the van. My dad was quite allergic to bees and maybe that's why he had wanted me out of the van. It was the only reason I could come up with. I grabbed my small denim purse and hopped down to the black paved driveway. My dad was still behind the van but met me as soon as I had closed the van door.

"There's a man sleeping in the back seat," he stated.

I began shaking and asked him, "What, a man...asleep in our van? I didn't see him, are you sure?"

My dad put his arm around me as I continued to shake and we both went inside our house. My dad phoned the police to report a man sleeping in our van. The officers arrived within ten minutes. They explained that there had been a robbery very close to our residence and perhaps this man was somehow involved and he decided to hideout in our vehicle.

I watched from the living room window as the police handcuffed the forlorn young man and placed him in their patrol car. We opened the key shop late that day. I was still shaken up from the event. Even today, I think this was one lesson learned that had a profound impact on my life. I had looked my dad straight in the eyes, with the man laying in the back seat, and didn't even see him.

Always listen to your parents. Even when you don't want to, listen to your parents. They know best. I share this story with my students as we approach the end of the school year. They're nearly teenagers then and often want more independence and less listening to their elders. For some strange reason, they still listen to my stories. I hope they learn from them.

I only made five dollars per week at my dad's bicycle and lock shop, not counting all of the food I ate during the week. When I reached seventy dollars in savings from my earnings, I opened my first savings account. I also purchased an initial pinky ring.

In the 60's, pinky rings and ID bracelets were quite popular. Girls wanted their pinky rings, so I had to have one in 14k gold. This was my first piece of jewelry. I still have it today. I've tried to slip it over my pinky finger, however, it only goes to above the knuckle and stops. It's dull and lacks the vibrant shine it once had. I can still see the cursive capital "D" embossed across the surface of it. Perhaps I should have it re-sized.

What still has meaning and needs no fitting, however, is the look on my dad' s face telling me to get out of the van. That will always fit. That will always have meaning to me. Over time, my students will learn to recognize tone of voice and the meanings that coincide with sounds. As said in the past and is still true today, parents know best. There is a time to question and a time to listen.

Chapter 15

JAKOB

Oh, the excitement of setting up a classroom for the new school year! You receive your student roster and look at the names, full of wonder and you search for identity. What will the students be like? How much fear will they have about attending a middle school? All of these questions and more capture my mind as I continue to browse the columns of unfamiliar names in search of a familiar family.

I come across one or two names that fill me with hope of a known family. And even if that student is from a family that I've already had in my class, I know this student will be unique. Still, joy fills my heart to be reunited with a past family once more.

"Mrs. Burggraaf, please report to the main office." The announcement echoed across campus over the intercom. It's the voice of the principal's secretary. When she writes a note requesting to see you, or does an "all-call" across the school, you respond.

I made the trek to the administrative offices and approached her office. Inside, she and another secretary had serious poses on their faces. I observed that each of them had copies of my classes in front of them. I was informed that they had a "special" student for me. Both of them had known the family quite well; the grandparents were dear friends.

"This young man is one of four children. He was left at his father's place of business by the mother and is now being raised by the dad. Mom took off with another guy and is now in Florida. There are four boys in the family and we thought about placing Jakob Kempleton in your classroom. This would provide him with a positive environment, being that he's been through so much," shared Mrs. Euland, practically in one full breath.

I froze. I looked into the secretary's eyes and shared, "Well, that's exactly what happened to me with my dad and my sister. My mom left and my dad had to raise us in our early years. I turned out alright..."

"We feel that Jakob will have stability and structure in your CORE classroom. It's low in numbers..." chimed in Mrs. Bartretti. I told both of them it would be my pleasure to have Jakob in my class and looked forward to meeting him tomorrow.

Usually, the students' schedules are computer generated, taking into consideration students with Individualized Learning Plans, 504's, Gifted, and English Language Learners. Often, it is a random placement that works out very well. Occasionally, due to parent requests or counselor's decisions, students are shifted and re-scheduled into more appropriate classrooms that will meet their needs.

Jakob walked into my portable, tall and lean with sea blue shifting eyes unsure of what was going to happen next. I approached him with a warm handshake to welcome him. He wouldn't look at me from day one. He would turn his head to the side and talk with a soft tone. I showed Jakob his seat with another boy and two girls.

He sat with his group but rarely wanted to participate in group tasks at first. Often, Jakob would have outbursts, where he acted as the class clown demanding acceptance from others. I interpreted this as a behavior he was acting out because he was suffering from the loss of his mother.

I didn't push Jakob into learning. I was simply there for Jakob. I knew he would come around when he was ready. Jakob just needed time to learn to have daily structure, and to know that I would be there every day in the classroom offering stability.

I was the missing link Jakob so craved in his daily life. I vowed to do my best. Throughout the school year, Jakob's teachers requested conferences. Often due to his behavior in school; other times a concern with incomplete assignments and homework. His dad was always there, willing and ready to support his son in any way he could.

I remember in one conference his dad, exhausted from work, sat slumped in his chair at the large oak table. I glanced at him and wondered how could he possibly do what he does? He was raising four boys by himself and working two jobs. And he has time for a conference?

And then I envisioned my dad sitting there, raising two girls, five and seven years old, by himself because my real mother had taken off with some guy named, "Frank."

I snapped back into the conference and listened to Jakob's dad speak, expressing his concerns. The other teacher shared as well. When it came time for me to speak, I enthusiastically shared my thoughts. "It was a very slow start for Jakob, but then he jumped right in and showed interest in reading and writing, especially writing." I felt this strategy was a great outlet for Jakob to have the opportunity to express himself and share with others. I explained that he had buckled down and the acting out in class had lessened. Additionally, I shared that getting homework from Jakob was a challenge, which showed on his progress reports and report cards.

I continued to speak with Jakob's dad throughout the year. He also visited the classroom for special events like Egyptian Day or Greek Olympics. His dad was out on disability due to a back injury that had occurred at work. I took away a renewed sense of strength from his dad's visits, that I in turn, gave back to my students in the classroom. It supported the loss of my own real mother, which at such a young age is difficult for any child. The concept is that if you never give up and try real hard, you will succeed.

Jakob and I never gave up hope. And it is that hope that we share with others who come in contact with our lives today. Our histories, though occurring at different times, were unfortunately replicable. And still are today. Right now, another mother or father is leaving the family behind for whatever reasons, and the ones left behind will struggle for a bit until they come in contact with someone who believes in them.

One person will be in their corner and cheer them on. One person will be there for them on a consistent basis. It doesn't matter if it is an aunt, a neighbor, a teacher, or a grandparent. You work with what you have and once again, you start believing, simply because someone genuinely cares for you.

At the end of the school year, I received a copy of a restraining order against the mom stating that she was allowed to visit Jakob, but she was not allowed to take him off campus. When I met her, our class was on the way to the school library to check out books. She joined in the line and we formally introduced ourselves as the students began to select books for checkout.

She sat across the table from me and expressed her concern about Jakob, inquired how he was doing in school, and wanted to know how she could help him.

All I could think to myself was, "You should have been there for Jakob, simply to love him." Somehow, I managed to share the week's writing prompt and that Jakob needed help editing his first draft. Jakob returned to our table and proudly took out the crumbled copy of his writing assignment and with pencil in hand, passed it to his mom.

It was as if a ghost had shown up; an old memory come alive again. Part of me was happy; the other part sad because I knew she would disappear from Jakob's life again and return at an unannounced moment for another snapshot in time.

My real mom phoned me when I was sixteen years old. I asked, "Who is this?"

"This is your mother," the unfamiliar gruff voice on the line replied.

I remember being in shock and then we talked mostly about the weather. I had nothing to say to her, this person who was now a stranger. I didn't want to know her; I had no place for her in my world. She had made the decision to leave two girls behind. Others had replaced her and became my world and they provided me with a positive, nurturing environment to grow up in. I hung up from her and never wanted to talk with her again. Nor did I.

Jakob completed sixth grade and entered

seventh grade in the fall. He seemed to be doing well and often visited my classroom and then would ask for a late pass. In eighth grade, he became my teacher's assistant, stapling papers for me or putting together reading logs. It was a pleasure to have him in class again.

Jakob had grown up and was now loved by those who were in his life. He no longer looked away with those ocean blue eyes; they now cast a warm glow of the swaying waves, frolicking in the sun and dancing at the shoreline. Jakob had a spark about him that was vibrant. He was now able to share his love with others and cared about himself enough to go forward in life with what he has.

It was the end of August and I was setting up my classroom when an announcement was made that our student class lists were in our teacher boxes. I dropped everything and started to walk up to the office, full of excitement. I sloped down to reach in my box for the stapled packets. As I strolled down the cement corridor returning to my classroom, I flipped through the pages, looking at the last names for familiar families. "Oh!" I stopped my walk.

"Kempleton, Joseph. Could it be?" I thought to myself. "Could this be Jakob's younger brother?" I wondered how his family was doing now. And a little glimpse from my past warmed my heart as I hoped it really was the same family. I was there for Jakob and now I'll be there for Joe.

Chapter 16

DAVID

I was in my early twenties when I met David. I was employed at a small key shop in Palm Springs, California and he worked for one of our suppliers for locksets, hardware, and key blanks. I looked forward to his visits each month and was filled with excitement to see him.

David was a quiet, soft-spoken gentleman. His salt and pepper beard draped over his Santa like cheeks and when he smiled, his soft blue eyes captured me. I couldn't wait for him to finish writing his order with my boss so that we had time to visit. We would talk about movies, relationships, travel, and restaurants. Often, we would enjoy lunch together at the small café next to the key shop. He would always order a big double cheeseburger with fries, and I'd have a green salad with crackers and a Coke. We loved visiting together, so much that we began to see each other outside of work.

David and I would go to dinner and sometimes see a movie. We loved going to the movies and ordering a large popcorn with extra butter. I wanted salt, so I would ask the cashier for a cardboard box. David would pour the popcorn into the box and then I shook the salt on top of the butter. In addition to going to the movies, David knew how much I loved to write. For years, I was a pencil to paper writer, as I did not own a computer.

In the evenings, I would go over to David's studio apartment. As I was greeted by this tall, handsome, intelligent man, I would hear the jazz station playing in the background. I would bring over my penciled rough draft from my night school college course and use his computer to write my papers.

We were always up for hours, reading and re-writing. David was my worst critic. He would take out that red pen and it seemed that every paper needed corrections. I felt frustration while writing, and learned through David that there really is no such thing as a final draft. David was hard on me. I thought I was a great writer and loved it, however, he would always find something that needed to be changed.

During my two ten week sessions of student teaching, David would help me write and assemble my student portfolios. I remember quite well when it was two in the morning, my eyes were sagging and I had no more brain cells left to think. David would push me to complete an as-

signment for my professor. He showed me how to organize binders with specific requirements of the course and he taught me presentation and design. I learned so much by him helping me.

During this time, we grew close to the point that I now had a key to his apartment. I remember one note he left me while he was at work. "Enjoy the fresh lemonade while you go for a swim today. Happy writing. Remember, a writer is an artist who paints a picture with words. Love, David."

I ended up moving into David's apartment and we became a couple. He filled my days with the warmth of the sunshine. Not one day passed when I didn't look forward to seeing him and being with him each night. I began student teaching in Oceanside, California and was a contracted teacher within two months. He was so proud of me and I was indebted to him for his wisdom and his writing skills. He knew that someday I really wanted to write children's books and supported me wholeheartedly.

Years passed together and we had finally planned a big trip to Maui. We had visited such places as Lake Tahoe and Las Vegas, but this was such a special trip because neither of us had been to a Hawaiian island. We had re-

served a condominium for one week and we were ready to go!

At the time, I was teaching Social Studies at Orange Grove Middle School and was enrolled in a two-week course studying Ancient China. It tied in perfectly with the sixth grade curriculum that included teaching the ancient civilizations. It was summertime and this workshop cost me nothing but gas money, as this was a grant course with an attractive stipend paid on the final day. We planned to take this money to Maui with us for our vacation.

It was July 18, 1996 when I arrived home at two-thirty in the afternoon. I opened the garage door with the clicker and went in. I noticed the answering machine flashing and pressed the red button to listen to the messages. As I listened, I heard, "This is the hospital and it's important for you to call us immediately." There were three of these messages. I couldn't imagine why the hospital wanted me to call.

Just then, the wife of David's business partner walked through the open door of the garage, crying and wiping her eyes. I asked, "What's wrong, what's going on?"

She murmured, "David, it's David," and was sobbing and shaking her head.

I asked, "David, your David?" Her husband's name was David, too.

"NO, your David, he had a heart attack, Deb, he didn't make it." She blurted out, now holding onto my body for comfort.

"What, what...what do you mean? He died? No way!" I was in disbelief and now squatting against the side of the kitchen counter. "No, no way, we're leaving for Maui in two days." I cried as I looked down the hallway at the packed luggage.

The phone rang again. It was the hospital to confirm the unthinkable news. My David did suffer from a massive heart attack and I needed to go to the hospital to identify the body. I hung up in shock and phoned my father. He told me that I needed to go to the hospital and call him from there and that he was on his way to Oceanside to be with me. I told him this couldn't be true.

I arrived at the hospital and somehow made it to the designated room. I entered in with a nurse to see David's lifeless body on a table, machines still attached to him and the flat line monitor still reflecting three cold green lines. The tubes were still in his mouth, so I kissed his bearded cheek. His hands were a combination of lavender and white. Buttons from his shirt were on the black and white linoleum floor and I picked them up. The doctors must have ripped them off quickly trying to keep David alive.

"The doctors did everything they could do to save him," the nurse shared softly. "They worked on him for thirty minutes..." she added.

It was over. My world came crashing down in an instant and would never be the same. I ran my shaking fingers over his body crying like a baby. "How could he leave me? He was everything to me."

I kissed him one final time and stepped outside of the room where I was asked to sit down. I asked the nurse, "What do I do, what happens next?"

I was looking for answers and there were none. I asked to use a telephone and called my father to confirm the devastating news. He was already driving to our home. I asked the nurse for a brochure or something to follow as a guide because I had no knowledge of what to do when someone dies. She had nothing to give me and informed me that the funeral home and the mortician will be in contact. She said what I needed to do now was to go home and get rest.

"Get rest?" I thought. "I can't even think. This

can't be happening; this isn't real."

I drove home in shock and looked at David's car in the driveway. "He'll be coming home soon," I thought.

I phoned my school principal, Dr. Barnes, and told her what had happened and that I was fine and she said, "No you're not, I'm on my way over."

Dr. Barnes had called a couple of colleagues from school and they walked in with a tray of cooked chicken, an assortment of cut cantaloupe, and a bottle of tequila. I think I nibbled on that chicken for nearly two weeks as I remember that was all I had eaten.

Each night, I sat in the dark living room and watched the car lights flash through the sliding glass door waiting for David to come home. David wasn't coming home anymore.

I went to my China course the next day and informed the professors about what had happened last night. They couldn't believe that I was even there. They told me that if I needed to step out during the class to make a phone call or two, that was fine. Both were very understanding and surprised that I had even returned to the course. David would have wanted me to finish the course. He had driven me into becoming a "doer" and not a "quitter."

There was no trip to Maui. There were no more dreams. I didn't have a writing critic anymore. I had no one to go to the movies with and eat buttery popcorn. There was no one to share my days with. My life had changed and this change took years to overcome. I'm not sure that I actually ever got over David's death. I miss him today and I'll miss him every tomorrow. I feel as though he is with me as I write each word and paragraph in this book.

Life does go on. You manage. Joy does return and you find peace and happiness again. My world had been rocked and yet I made it as I continued to climb each mountain and not stop until I reached the top.

I have David to thank for this. He was my love, my partner, and my dear friend. I will miss him forever. I had a person who believed in me and taught me so much. I hope this part of me is shared with my students on a daily basis.

Today, I take my time and help my students organize their binders or clean out their backpacks. I help edit their writing and assist when selecting word replacement. I show them how to prioritize their projects for classes. I encourage students to approach writing as a process; that there really is no such thing as a final draft. All of these skills and more, are an extension of David's teaching to me.

And so, David does live on. I can feel those soft blues eyes stare at me once again and my heart continues to melt.

Chapter 17

SUZIE'S DAD

Middle school students are so young when they enter this big new college-like campus. It's such a new world for them with so many freedoms. They have to pass each period to their next class. Likewise, they must learn to manage their time in order to stop at their lockers and visit with friends. Their lunches consist of "a la carte" hot items with tasty popular treats, such as pizza and nachos. Additionally, students have the opportunity to select their elective courses.

Every nine weeks classes rotate and the students have many options when it comes to choosing their elective classes including art, music, gym or drama. In addition, the students can choose to serve as an office assistant. More often than not, these youngsters love coming to middle school and welcome the change from being in a small school as they delve into their big new world.

Suzie was a quiet girl with soft flowing shoulder length hair. Her skin was a sun grazed bronze and when I looked at her in class, I often thought she could be a famous model one day. She was very humble and talked with a soft tone at her table. Her assignments were always complete, neat, and done very well.

Each month in Language Arts classes, teachers receive thin book order forms from large companies to distribute to students. The kids make their selections and return their book order forms by the required date and wait for their orders to arrive. Usually, each company has a special offer that allows students to purchase a book for only ninety-nine cents! This is such a deal and I encourage the students to buy at least one book for their weekly home reading log assignment. Finally, these companies make it financially easier for teachers to build up their classroom libraries with such specials offered each month.

After I distribute the tissue-like colorful order forms to the students, the classroom is filled with chatter and discussion of novels and authors. I have two wire baskets on the table where I place additional order forms in case the students lose theirs or they need more forms. Next, I hang a large manila folder on the ledge of the whiteboard where students place their orders. It's wonderful to hear the kids so excited about reading.

After the students were dismissed and busses revved off campus, I was changing my boards for the next day. I change the date along with the following day's assignment. I also put up the *Quote for the Day* and the starter sentence for the response. I do this because the start of each school morning is hectic enough so I'd much rather do it after school each day.

As I gathered my briefcase and tote bag and approached the door to leave, I heard a firm knock. I opened the door to see Suzie and her father standing there. I smiled and welcomed them both in. Suzie had red rings around her brown eyes as if she had been crying. Her dad's face was full of anger.

"Mrs. Burggraaf, when I was picking Suzie up in front of the school, she told me that you made her feel bad. I don't think it's part of a teacher's job to make kids feel bad when they're in school."

My mouth dropped and I was stunned. What had I said...what did I do? I thought to myself as I quickly reflected over class that day.

"Oh, I don't know what happened sir, please let me know what happened! She's such a nice girl and a pleasure to have in class," I managed to utter with concern and worry.

"When you were handing out the book orders, you skipped her. Her feelings were hurt. Suzie raised her hand to tell you but you did nothing about it," he added.

My mouth dropped along with my heart. How could I have skipped her? I didn't see her hand raised. How could I have missed her? The students know where the extra forms are kept. Why didn't she just get up and get one? Even on her way out of class, she could have taken one from the basket.

So many thoughts were rushing through my head. Now, Suzie was crying like a summer shower in Florida. All this sadness and anger over a book order. How could I make a student feel so badly by forgetting her?

I walked over to where Suzie was sitting, with tears still streaming down her face. "Suzie, here, here are two book orders; one from each company. Please forgive me for not giving them to you. I never meant to skip you."

"Thank you, Mrs. Burggraaf," Suzie managed to choke out over her sadness.

"Please, Suzie, don't be sad. It was my mistake," I blurted out as my eyes started to fill with tears.

"Thank you, Mrs. Burggraaf," Suzie's dad continued. "I really don't like seeing my daughter so upset. Thank you for giving her the book orders." He spoke with a little more ease and satisfaction.

Suzie stood up next to her dad. I shook his hand and they both left. I sat down. After what I thought was a great day at school, I now felt terrible. Somehow, I gathered my belongings once more and locked my portable. I walked to my car as if I was in the clouds. I felt so sad that I had forgotten Suzie.

The next day, my principal saw me checking my box and asked to see me briefly before I went to my room. I went in and sat down across from her desk. She said she had received a note from a father yesterday regarding his daughter being upset.

My heart sank once more. I explained to my principal about the book orders being passed out and how I had neglected to issue one to his daughter. I also explained that he came to see me after school and I offered my apology for making Suzie feel so bad.

My principal leaned forward in her familiar warm stance with her elbows on her knees and her face close to mine. "Deb, I know you care for your students, each one of them, and that this was an oversight. Please don't let this bother you. You did your best. Thank you for talking with the father after school."

I stood up to start my day and felt like a rubber Gumby all over again. Today, I thought, I will not forget one student. I don't care if it's passing out papers, reading packets, or handouts from the office, I will not forget a single student.

Suzie and her dad had an impact on my teaching for the rest of my career. Today, as I pass out the book order forms, I now tell the class, "If you did not receive one, please raise your hand." This will ensure that every student will be included.

Time passed and the day before winter break, Suzie placed a wrapped gift on my desk. It was a white coffee mug adorned with red roses and green leaves. Inside, was an assortment of delicious chocolates in red and silver wrappers. A lovely note from Suzie's mother and father read, "Thank you for being the best teacher Suzie has ever had. We appreciate all you do."

I still have that note in my Special Memories folder tucked away to reminisce about years past. I use the special coffee mug each day during the school year in honor of her and as a symbol to remember every child each day. What a beautiful way to start the day; a rose bouquet from Suzie.

Chapter 18

MOMMY

My mom became my mother when my dad married her in 1964. My real mother had left my younger sister and I to be raised by a single working father.

We lived in a small single wide trailer in a mobile home park. I remember when my dad started dating "Kathi." I didn't like her. I would lay in my upper bunk bed above my sister and listen to them talk at the small kitchen dinette set. Then they would go outside to talk and try to have privacy and I would peek out the small aluminum framed kitchen window and see them kissing in the front seat of the car.

I knew my dad had fallen in love and instead of being happy for him, I was angry. I didn't want another mother who would leave us again. I was perfectly happy with just the three of us as a family. Now, there was this intruder.

They dated for a period of time and then they married. I remember thinking, "I'm not calling her mom...she'll never be my mother."

For a very long time, I rebelled. I felt as

though I was always fighting her, no matter what it was about. We couldn't agree on anything; everything was a problem.

I wondered if my dad thought the transition for his two girls ultimately accepting a woman into their lives would be a lot smoother. Perhaps he thought because we were young, we would adapt easily. However for me, it was a rough transition and we butted heads all the way.

This caused problems for the relationship. It seemed my dad was always on our side. Kathi could never take a stand or reinforce the points she was trying to teach us. My sister and I had learned quickly to run to Dad when we needed something. We agreed not to ask Kathi because the answer would be no. This became a problem for my dad as he began to take sides.

I remember coming home after school one day to find my clothes dumped on top of my bedspread. Kathi said all of the items had to be refolded as they were not neat enough.

There were other times when I wanted to go places with my friends and she put her foot down and said," no." On the other hand, she allowed us to go to the movies on Sundays after church and gave each of us a quarter for popcorn. One afternoon, I had snuck into the R-rated movie, "Summer of 42," and Kathi found out. Of course, I was grounded. Kathi was simply doing her best at being an instant mom, and we were children, always ready to challenge.

Although the making of a new family was a rough road, both of my parents provided us with wonderful times together as we grew up. We had fantastic ski trips to Weston, Vermont. Kathi taught me how to snow ski and put me in private lessons with Uli, a top ski guru from Sweden. She taught me how to make scrumptious salads and how to decorate the table for dinners. At Cape Cod during the summers, we would cohog at Buzzards Bay. Kathi showed me how to keep the clams that were larger than an inch and a half and how to toss the small clams back into the bay.

We did so many things as a family, however, there was one day that is quite vivid. I cannot remember what happened, but we were over at my Aunt Ruth and Uncle Red's house. I was on the gray porch steps and looked up at her and called her, "Mom." This was a defining moment for both of us because for the first time since she had become our step-mother, I was finally giving her the respect and love she deserved.

From that moment, she was my mother.

There is no one else; I don't even acknowledge her as my step-mom. When we meet people, they comment on how much I look like her. We both smile at each other.

Today, my mom is my best friend. She is the one person with whom I can share anything with and still be accepted and loved. She adores me and I respect her and love her sincerely. I cannot thank her enough for never giving up on me and always being my, "Rock of Gibraltar."

Mommy lives in Connecticut during the summers and in her Florida condominium during the winter months. This is where her children and grandchildren are now. She loves being with all of us and sometimes she spends the night. We enjoy going out to dinner and then shopping together. I absolutely have a ball with my mom and can hardly wait for each winter for her to return so she will be near me again. I love our time together, except that it goes by too fast.

Thank you, Mom, for never giving up on me and believing in me. Thank you for always being by my side, laughing and crying with me, and being my confidant. More importantly, thank you for being my one and only Mother.

Chapter 19

SPRING BREAK

For five consecutive school years, I have taken students to Washington, D.C. during Spring Break. This was an educational tour for students that generated tremendous parent support and involvement.

During the month of April, I would hold parent meetings to discuss the Spring Break trip. A major concern for many parents was safety and I would reassure my parents that their child's safety was my number one priority. I assured them that the students are never alone; they are paired with another student throughout the entire trip.

Next, I discussed the highlights of the trip following the itinerary provided in the brochure from the travel company. We would visit the Tomb of the Unknown Soldier at Arlington, the Federal Bureau of Engraving and Printing, the White House, the FBI Building, the Mall which included the Air and Space Museum, the Iwo Jima Memorial, along with the Jefferson and Lincoln Memorials. It was a jam-packed tour. Our days started at seven o'clock for breakfast in the hotel and ended at ten-thirty at night when we would return back to our resting place.

Each year I would have nearly twenty middle school students and three parents that served as chaperones. I was so thankful to have my parents there to keep an eye on the students and help answer questions, provide snacks and assist when doing the counts at each meeting point. The parents were an outstanding asset.

The students always started the trek to D.C. full of energy and enthusiasm. By the second day of the trip, the students were beginning to tire by midday. They wanted to return to the hotel, change into their swimsuits and chill in the cool pool. Additionally, the students wanted to roam around the hotel and use the elevator. They always seemed to enjoy that. Finally, they just wanted to return to their rooms and order pizza to enjoy with their friends.

However, the students had a planned agenda which they needed to follow. First, we would tour the National Cathedral, the sixth largest Gothic cathedral in the world. Following this, we headed off to Arlington Cemetery which included loads of walking. In the afternoon, we had a scheduled time of two o'clock to place the wreath on the Tomb of the Unknown Soldier. At night, we visited the Iwo Jima Memorial. The pepperoni and cheese orders would have to wait until tomorrow night when we had more leisure time at the hotel.

The students and parents alike were quite tired. We stopped for dinner at a restaurant where the students could use their meal vouchers to select a meal of their choice. We only had forty-five minutes at this small mall, so if the students wanted to look around a little bit, they would have to eat quickly in order to shop.

It was now dusk and students met on time at the designated art structure at the top of the escalator near the mall's entrance. All were accounted for. We loaded our tour bus and off we went, first to the monuments, followed by Iwo Jima.

The students were in awe at the size of the Lincoln Memorial. It truly was mesmerizing at night. There must have been thousands of students viewing this sight. It was nearly impossible to know exactly where all of the students were at one time. However, this is why the students were paired in groups of two, along with a parent for each group. I kept reassuring myself silently that all of the students would return because it was easy to be overwhelmed with the amount of tourists on this evening tour.

Again, every student was accounted for at eight-thirty and we were now off to see the Iwo Jima Memorial. Our tour bus slowly drove around this massive art structure. Our tour guide noted that as we drove around the memorial and kept our eyes on the flag, it would seem as if the flag was being raised.

It's true! It's quite spectacular to see. After going around this wonderful piece of art, we were allowed outside of the bus for thirty minutes to walk and purchase souvenirs and to enjoy a soft drink, water, or lemonade. The students looked forward to these breaks and the social time. The adults needed a break as well.

We returned to Bus 403 at nine-thirty and did our student count. Everyone was accounted for. Just then, Steve asked me if he could go to the rear of the bus and sit with the group of students from New Mexico. I said that was fine and thanked him for asking me. I knew where he was, even though I had broken up our school group. Steve was now seated with the group from Albuquerque.

Shortly after, I heard, "Mrs. Burggraaf, Steve is not on this bus!"

“Yes, he is! We did our count when we boarded, everyone is here!”

Another student blurted out, “Mrs. Burggraaf, Steve is *not* on this bus, really!”

I stood up, holding onto the metal hand rail and looked for Steve out of sixty-five students and three schools combined on Bus 403. I didn’t see Steve’s brown curly hair and gold-framed glasses. I turned to the bus driver and firmly said, “Please stop the bus, we’re missing a student!”

The bus driver slowly pulled off to the right and stopped. Running along the left side of the bus were the familiar brown curls looking up to the steamed window panes of the bus. It was Steve.

I stepped out of the bus to meet him as I could feel his breath from panting and racing to catch up to the bus.

“Where were you? How come you weren’t with your partner?”

“I tried to catch up, Mrs. Burggraaf. I was the last one to pay for my soda and had to go to the bathroom. When I came out of the bathroom, my partner was gone, so I ran to the bus and it was gone, too!” He was panting while trying to talk and breathe at the same time.

"It's okay, Steve, just catch your breath, you're here now and we're together," I consoled him as he climbed into the bus. I looked Steve in the eyes to reassure him that he was back with us and everything was okay. He was still trying to catch his breath.

We both took our seats on the bus and I now had to catch my breath. I had lost my first student. I really thought he was on the bus. I must have counted a student from one of the other schools in *our* group count.

I attempted to slow my heartbeat down on the way back to the hotel. I needed a nice, hot shower and tomorrow I would be rested and full of energy again. I wouldn't let this happen again and would make sure my student count was accurate.

At the hotel, I had a meeting to attend before enjoying my nice retreat. It was only a twenty minute meeting where the chaperones meet together and go over the itinerary for the next day and make any changes as needed. We were provided nuts and fruits, along with a selection of juices and soft drinks. What a warm welcome after a long day with the kids.

But what a terrific time we had! On my way to my hotel room I saw a couple of students in the elevator and they said, "Thanks for a great day, Mrs. Burggraaf!"

"I'm glad you enjoyed the tours," I responded. "Tomorrow's a full day so you'd better get some rest tonight. I'll call your rooms tomorrow morning at six o'clock and we will meet for breakfast at seven o'clock sharp."

With that final note, the elevator door opened and I walked down the hallway to my room. I plopped on the bed with my backpack and turned on the television to view the local news. It was past eleven and I was exhausted. I showered, turned my bed down, set my alarm for five-thirty, and went off to dream land. I looked forward to another fun day with the students.

Chapter 20

THE ART AWARD

I was in ninth grade and a freshman at Danbury High School. My parents were in the middle of a bitter divorce. At times during school, I found it difficult to focus, especially when I got home to do my homework.

My heart wasn't into my assignments at that time. I was more focused on whether or not my family was going to stay together or my dad, sister, and I were going to head west to California.

I remember having a writing assignment for Mr. Gilgallon in Social Studies. I had selected Hitler for my research project and was given more than a month for this written assignment. I checked out library books on my topic, had all of the supplies at home to do it, however, I could not buckle down and write it completely. I remember turning it in to Mr. Gilgallon along with a note; "I'm sorry, I'm having family problems at home and was unable to finish."

He wrote back, "Hang in there," and graciously awarded me an undeserving "C" on my assignment. It brought my grade average down to a B, but with everything going on, I was happy with that.

Following this assignment, I remembered that the awards ceremony for "Most Outstanding Students" were a week away. All students, by grade level, were brought into the navy blue and gold decorated auditorium for this big school event. I went in and sat with my homeroom class, which was Art.

I had really enjoyed art this year with Mr. Schwartz. He was outstanding! He wasn't your "normal" art teacher; he made your creative side come alive and forced you to think out-of-the-box. At this time in my life with family concerns, I never realized the affect this class had on me.

One project Mr. Schwartz assigned to us was to create three dimensional objects that would be edible. Well, not really edible, but they had to be a food product. You had to be able to hold it in your hands and it had to look real.

I made a bowl full of fruit and a pepperoni pizza. For the bowl of fruit, I took a large balloon and layered half of it with newspaper strips soaked in flour and water. I draped them haphazardly over the balloon trying to create an even "thickness" of my bowl. When it dried, I evenly cut out the edge of the bowl along its cir-

cumference and sanded it lightly after it dried with a fine grit sanding paper. I painted my bowl in a basket weave pattern with browns and yellow, making a gold color.

Next, for the fruit, I shaped the strips of newspaper into a banana. I made little balls of floured newspaper into grapes, and then painted them purple. Finally, I made apples with my flour and water mixture and painted them a red color tainted with yellow accents. My bowl of fruit was spectacular and would dazzle any kitchen counter.

For my pizza, I continued to work with flour, water, and newspaper making a thick, flat circle on top of a cut-out circle of hard cardboard. This took quite awhile to dry so I began to make my little circular pepperonis, cheese chunks, and tomato pieces out of floured newspaper and set them aside to dry. This was a two week project and took my family problems off my mind. It allowed me to escape into a more creative world.

When my pizza parts were nearly dry, I painted them with red, brown, and orange poster paints and blended the colors as best as I could to get the tones to the most "real" shades of food as possible. I brought my project into class and Mr. Schwartz said that I had done a remarkable job. We all shared our art projects with the class. I received an "A."

I was thinking of this project as students were seated in the plush cushioned seats. After the principal was introduced and we saluted the flag, the awards ceremony began. First, the core subjects were awarded in ninth grade. Following this were gym, drama, music, and art. I sat with my friends and applauded the students who were receiving this honor.

"Mr. Schwartz, will you please step forward to present the Art Award to the Most Outstanding Student of the Year," the ninth grade counselor instructed.

Mr. Schwartz came forward and said, "It is with great honor that this year's award goes to a ninth grader of whom I am very proud of, Deborah Van Houten."

I was in my seat and had just heard my name. It was me! "Oh my goodness!" I thought, "I have to go down to the front of the stage in front of all of these people."

I remember everyone clapping as I headed for Mr. Schwartz, climbing the five steps on the left side of the stage. He was a stout, jolly man that carried a wide smile. He always wore a suit and tie and looked more like a television news announcer than an art teacher. His smile stretched across his face as he extended his hand to shake mine. I could still hear the clapping as I saw the gleam in his eyes.

I was issued a small lapel pin, half inch by half inch made of brass. Diagonally across it in capital navy blue letters, read, "HONOR." On either side of this word is an open book and a lantern of knowledge with a sun beaming from its left side.

The applause subsided and I hurried back to my seat in the rear of the auditorium, looking for a familiar face as I was still surprised to receive this award. Mr. Schwartz hadn't told me; my parents didn't say a word. Yet, I was deeply honored.

Now-a-days, I shy away from the newspaper, flour, and water mixture. I think I had enough of it in ninth grade. But it was a lot of fun, as well as creative and therapeutic. Today, I enjoy working with watercolor and Indian ink. I love how the watercolor blends. At times, you don't have control over it. After it dries, I enjoy adding the details with the Indian ink. These vibrant colors provide the accents that make the art come alive.

I think every child should have the opportu-

nity to work with flour, water, and newspaper to create unique pieces of art. Moreover, I hope every student has the chance to have such an inspirational teacher who has the ability to take you to another place, outside of your own world and allow you to discover that space for yourself.

Chapter 21

FRENCH TOAST

It was late on a Friday afternoon and students had just completed Diagnostic Testing in their morning classes. They were exhausted. All they wanted to do was put their heads down in the afternoon and rest. Some of them wanted to draw.

In my Language Arts classes, I had issued a *Book Report Poster* project earlier in the week. I thought this was a great opportunity for students to lay out their design including specific requirements, but I had to make it fun for them.

I issued small 2 x 2 orange and pink post-it stickers to each collaborating group of students. On white paper, the students placed the stickers containing the components of the report: *title of book, author, character, plot, symbol, vocabulary, theme and mood.* Next, I encouraged students to draw certain scenes from their books that they would like to include on their posters.

Students were very excited about this art lesson. It seemed to keep the students engaged on literary elements after a long day of testing. As I walked around the classroom to guide students and answer questions, I heard a couple of giggles from Team One in the front of the classroom.

"Look, Mrs. B, look at Jimmy!" The kids continued laughing from across the classroom. As I approached this table of four students, I, too, had a chuckle in my heart.

"Mrs. Burggraaf, Jimmy is asleep!" Shelbea shared.

Jimmy had taken two of the orange post-it stickers and drew the circumference of eyes on each of them. Next, he darkened two black pupils in the centers of the eyes. Then, he placed the orange eyes on top of his eye brows, folded his arms on his desk and put his head down and went to sleep. He was exhausted from testing. Here was this quiet, creative student with orange post-it eyes sleeping in my class during period six.

"Jimmy, time to wake up, it's almost time for dismissal," I said softly.

"Sorry, Mrs. Burggraaf. I am so tired." Jimmy lifted his head, pulling off his orange eyes and rubbing his head.

"It's okay," I comforted. "You kids have had a lot of testing over the past two days. I know you're very drained. Here, take these stickers home and over the weekend when you're rested, you can design your project."

Jimmy accepted the *post-its* and added, "I was dreaming about French toast, Mrs. Burggraaf. With lots of maple syrup. And butter, too."

"What a sweet dream, Jimmy. Maybe you can enjoy French toast with your family this weekend. It sounds delicious," I said.

The dismissal bell rang and students packed up their backpacks and were on their way out the door. As I straightened the team desks, my mind drifted off to Jimmys' buttery French toast.

My Uncle Joe was famous for making us French toast on the weekend. Sometimes Lynn and Joann would spend the night at our house. Often, I would have the opportunity to go over and stay at their house.

Their father was my fun uncle who loved me unconditionally. Uncle Joe would set Lynn and I up in the basement with delicious treats and make the room real dark for us. We would watch scary movies all afternoon and into the evenings. We would enjoy popcorn and candy and sometimes Uncle Joe would have to wake us and put us to bed.

Sunday mornings live on today. Nobody made French toast like Uncle Joe. He would dip each white slice of bread into the egg, milk, vanilla extract, and cinnamon mixture until it was real soggy. Next, he placed the bread into the sizzling buttered pan, slice by slice. The cinnamon wafted across the kitchen as Lynn and I sat awaiting our delicious treat.

"How many more, Deb?" Uncle Joe would ask as he served our breakfast fit for two queens.

"I think I can eat two more, Uncle Joe." I chewed slowly on this soft, soggy, sweet delicacy. Uncle Joe didn't make his French toast brown and dry; but soggy and moist and succulent. Lynn and I just kept adding swirls of Vermont maple syrup. This truly was the highlight of our weekends together.

Uncle Joe passed in November of 2007. He was a special person in my life—a kooky kind of man with a wit that always made people laugh. He said what was on his mind and was one of the most caring people who have touched my life. We spent a lot of time together as I was growing up. We enjoyed weekends in the summer, swimming in the pool. In the winter, we were skiing the powdery white slopes in Weston, Vermont. I remember Uncle Joe made up crazy words and always made us laugh even though we didn't understand everything.

"Ahhhh, minka," echoed in my mind as I drove off from school thinking about Uncle Joe's words and Thomas, with his French toast dream dripping behind orange post-it eyes.

My sugary weekends went with me as I left the school campus for the weekend. Perhaps I'll make French toast this Sunday. But it won't be as good as my Uncle Joe's. He was just that sugary kind of guy...

CONTACT INFORMATION

Thank you for reading **Caught In The Middle.** If you would like to share your comments about the book or to order additional books, the contact information is as follows. I look forward to hearing from you.

Thank you

Deborah Burggraaf

Deborah Burggraaf

Address: 7040 Seminole Pratt Whitney Road, Suite 25-152

Loxahatchee, FL 33470

Email: deb@dburgg.com

Website: www.dburgg.com